THE NEW BIBLE CURE FOR SLEEP DISORDERS

DON COLBERT, MD

SILOAM

Most CHARISMA HOUSE BOOK GROUP products are available at special quantity discounts for bulk purchase for sales promotions, premiums, fund-raising, and educational needs. For details, write Charisma House Book Group, 600 Rinehart Road, Lake Mary, Florida 32746, or telephone (407) 333-0600.

THE NEW BIBLE CURE FOR SLEEP DISORDERS by Don Colbert, MD
Published by Siloam
Charisma Media/Charisma House Book Group
600 Rinehart Road
Lake Mary, Florida 32746
www.charismahouse.com

Unless otherwise noted, all Scripture quotations are from the New Living Translation of the Bible, copyright © 1996, 2004. Used by permission of Tyndale House Publishers, Inc., Wheaton, IL 60189. All rights reserved.

Scripture quotations marked KJV are from the King James Version of the Bible.

Scripture quotations marked NAS are from the New American Standard Bible, copyright © 1960, 1962, 1963, 1968, 1971, 1972, 1973, 1975, 1977, 1995 by the Lockman Foundation. Used by permission. (www. Lockman.org)

Scripture quotations marked NKJV are from the New King James Version of the Bible. Copyright © 1979, 1980, 1982 by Thomas Nelson, Inc., publishers. Used by permission.

Copyright © 2009 by Don Colbert, MD
All rights reserved

Library of Congress Cataloging in Publication
Colbert, Don.
  The new Bible cure for sleep disorders / by Don Colbert.
      p. cm.
  Includes bibliographical references.

ISBN 978-1-59979-758-8

1. Sleep disorders--Religious aspects--Christianity. I. Title.
RC547.C653 2009
616.8'498--dc22

2009033713

14 15 16 17 18 — 10 9 8 7 6 5 4
Printed in the United States of America

CONTENTS

INTRODUCTION
A BRAND-NEW BIBLE CURE
FOR A BRAND-NEW YOU!..............................1

Sleep Disorders... 3

My Own Story 3

A Bold, New Approach..................................... 6

1 REST ASSURED—YOU CAN FIND REST!.......9

Understanding Sleep Deprivation 10

Sleep Debt 12

Dangers of Too Little Sleep 13

Dangers of Too Much Sleep.................................... 15

Sleep Requirements During the Stages of Life 17

Sleep Architecture 18

Sleep Diary 20

Conclusion 22

2 REST ASSURED BY BEING INFORMED
ABOUT SLEEP DISORDERS 25

The Nightmare of Insomnia.................................... 26

   Primary insomnia.................................... 26

   Secondary insomnia.................................... 26

Sleep Apnea.. 27

Symptoms 28

Obstructive sleep apnea 29

Central sleep apnea................................ 31

Mixed sleep apnea 32

Does Your Partner's Snoring Keep You Awake?..... 32

Narcolepsy... 35

Insomnia and Movement Disorders..................... 36

Restless legs syndrome (RLS) 36

Periodic limb movement disorder (PLMD) 38

Circadian Rhythms 39

Problems Within Circadian Rhythms 40

Night owls 40

Early birds 42

Jet lag.. 42

Shift work 43

Artificial light pollution 44

Parasomnias.. 45

Night terrors... 45

Nightmares... 46

Sleepwalking 47

Sleep-related eating disorder.................. 48

Bruxism.. 48

REM sleep behavior disorder 49

See Your Doctor..50

Conclusion 50

3 REST ASSURED THROUGH PROPER NUTRITION 53

Eating to Help Get Your Rest 53

Caffeine 54

Sleep Soundly With Less Sugar and
Fewer Carbs 55

Late-Night Eating and Drinking........................... 57

Maintaining Your Ideal Weight........................... 58

Conclusion 59

4 REST ASSURED THROUGH GOOD HEALTH HABITS................................ 61

Are You Losing Sleep Over Stress? 61

Aerobic Exercise 62

Sleep Hygiene 63

Conclusion 66

5 REST ASSURED THROUGH PROACTIVE SLEEP THERAPIES.................... 69

Light Up Your Life!.. 69

Light Therapy for Improving Sleep....................... 70

Night-shift workers.. 71

The Power of Napping 72

Other Sleep Therapies 73

　Cognitive-behavioral therapy (CBT) 73

　Progressive muscle relaxation 75

　Abdominal breathing............................ 75

　Visual imagery and/or meditation 75

　Biofeedback 76

Conclusion.. 77

6 REST ASSURED THROUGH
　SUPPLEMENTS...79

Supplements for Sound Sleep 79

　A good multivitamin/multimineral supplement.... 80

　Melatonin 80

　L-tryptophan and 5-HTP (5-hydroxytryptophan).... 81

　L-theanine and GABA 82

　Magnesium... 83

　Other teas to treat insomnia 84

　Valerian root.. 85

　Magnolia bark and adaptogens 85

　Progesterone.. 86

Supplements for Other Sleep Disorders.............. 87

　Restless legs syndrome 87

　Periodic limb movement disorder 87

Should I Ask My Doctor for Medications
for Sleep? 88

Conclusion 89

7 REST ASSURED THROUGH
   REST IN GOD 91

   Abiding in the Word of God 92

   Understanding and Obeying the Law of Rest....... 93

A PERSONAL NOTE From Don Colbert 97

APPENDIX A
   CONFESSIONS FOR SLEEP...........................99

APPENDIX B
   RESOURCES FOR SLEEP DISORDERS 103

NOTES...105

A BRAND-NEW BIBLE CURE
FOR A BRAND-NEW YOU!

I F SLEEP DISORDERS have left you feeling exhausted, depleted, and defeated, rest assured that these things are not God's will for you. You can discover real rest and wonderful refreshing in God. "Then Jesus said, 'Come to me, all of you who are weary and carry heavy burdens, and I will give you rest. Take my yoke upon you. Let me teach you, because I am humble and gentle at heart, and you will find rest for your souls. For my yoke is easy to bear, and the burden I give you is light'" (Matt. 11:28–30).

God never intended for you to push through your days and months feeling increasingly weary. If you are struggling with sleep disorders, there's hope! Let's take a look.

The benefits to your body and mind of plenty of restful sleep cannot be measured. Sleep is absolutely vital to your health and well-being. During sleep you actually recharge your mind and body. Sleep allows your body to recuperate and restore itself from exhaustion. In addition, during sleep your cells are able to regenerate and rejuvenate because the body secretes growth hormones as you slumber that signal it to repair tissues and organs.

Sleep also gives your mind a mental break, and it helps to restore your memory. Dreaming helps your mind to sort out and resolve emotional conflicts. During sleep, your body rebuilds and removes toxins. As you rest your body mentally and physically, your energy is increased.

We spend up to one-third of our lives asleep, so getting adequate rest is critical for our health. Without enough sleep, the body begins to degenerate more rapidly. Adequate sleep actually helps to lower cortisol, the stress hormone. If our brains are deprived of sleep over the long term, brain aging results.

Sleep deprivation and excessive fatigue can actually lead to anxiety, depression, and extreme irritability, and they can cause you to gain weight. Lack of sleep can also dramatically undermine your immune system, which leads to more colds, flu, and other infectious diseases.

Fatigue will also lead to impaired mental function, causing problems at work or at school. The sleep-deprived tend to be more forgetful and less able to concentrate and focus. Decreased eye/hand coordination can result in a higher incidence of accidents and motor vehicle accidents. Tragically, about one hundred thousand accidents each year—resulting in nearly fifteen hundred deaths—are caused by people falling asleep at the wheel.[1]

If you wake up never feeling rested and refreshed, you may be sleeping enough hours but have poor sleep quality that is robbing your body and mind of much-needed rest. Or if you drag through your days feeling tired and spend too many nights staring at the ceiling or wandering around your house, you may be one of millions of Americans who suffer from a sleep disorder.

SLEEP DISORDERS

Sleep disorders are at epidemic levels in the United States. An estimated forty million Americans suffer from insomnia and other sleep disorders. Other reports state that 60 percent of American adults suffer from insomnia at least a few times each week. As a result, more than half of the population will experience daytime drowsiness.[2]

The average adult sleeps about seven to seven and a half hours a night during the workweek. Sleep requirements vary from individual to individual. Some people are able to function well on five hours of sleep a night, while others require nine hours a night. The key is how you feel when you wake up and how alert you feel throughout the day. If you do not wake up feeling refreshed, and if you get sleepy during the day, you may be experiencing a sleep disorder.

A recent survey revealed that approximately 40 percent of all adults claimed they were so drowsy that it interfered with their daily activities. More than half of the American adult population experiences drowsiness during the day.[3]

These statistics may seem shocking, but sleep disorders don't have to happen to you! Many individuals live with insomnia, restless sleep, fatigue, and mental cloudiness for years, believing that sleep disorders are something they must accept. But that is simply not true!

MY OWN STORY

Let me share my own personal story. In medical school, internship, and residency, as well as in private practice, I had to learn how to function on little to no sleep. During internship in family medicine, I was on call every fourth night, and when on call, I rarely slept more than one to two hours and then had to work the entire next day. Some nights when I was on call I was up literally all night and the next day.

At first, it was easy, but as months turned into years, I began to get fatigued. During residency, I was on call about one time a week. After finishing internship and residency, I went into solo practice, and you guessed it, I was on call every night. The first year or so it was not bad because I did not have that many patients; sometimes I would go one or two weeks without a page after hours. However, as my practice grew, my nighttime pages and calls increased, and I began to be awakened about every night. This went on for years, and as my nighttime calls steadily increased, my energy decreased.

I had increased irritability and fatigue, and it became more and more difficult to concentrate. I also became more forgetful. Some mornings my wife would ask me who had called in the middle of the night and awakened us, and I would look at her with uncertainty on my face. I had actually forgotten who had called and whether or not I had phoned in a prescription and even what the prescription was. Research now shows that just one sleepless night can impair driving performance as much as an alcohol blood level of 0.10 percent, which is higher than the legal limit for driving.[4]

I literally became so fatigued that I had to put my car in park when I stopped at a red light because I feared I would fall asleep at the light. I would even fall asleep shortly after a movie would start, even though I would really want to see the movie. I would also nearly fall asleep on a forty-minute drive to the beach even with my wife talking to me. I was truly sleep deprived.

As I became more and more fatigued, my immune system began to suffer, and I suffered from recurrent colds, flu, and sinus infections. I also developed irritable bowel syndrome with abdominal bloating, abdominal pains, and bouts of diarrhea. As my lack of sleep continued, I eventually developed psoriasis and chronic fatigue.

This was in the late 1980s; I had not been trained yet in nutrition, so I turned to taking antibiotics. I would recover, but a month or so later I would get another infection and take another round of antibiotics. From lack of sleep my immune system had become impaired.

In search of answers for my own health problems, I spent the next few years learning nutrition, detoxification, and a healthy diet, as well as the importance of stress reduction and dealing with deadly emotions. However, I did not regain my health until I began getting adequate restorative sleep and repaying the sleep debt I had accrued.

You see, lack of sleep had impaired my alertness, work performance, concentration, and memory, and I eventually lost my health from lack of sleep. Here I was, only in my early thirties, and I had sacrificed my health by choosing to be on call and not getting adequate amounts of good, restful sleep.

Finally, I woke up to the fact that my main problem was lack of adequate restful sleep, and I then began to share calls with other physicians. Eventually I stopped taking night calls altogether. Making sleep a priority, going to bed at about the same time each night, waking up at about the same time each morning, and not being awakened during the night enabled me to repay the tremendous sleep debt that I had accumulated and thus regain my health.

A BOLD, NEW APPROACH

I was able to regain my health through proper rest, and you can too. With the help of the practical and faith-inspiring wisdom contained in this Bible Cure book, you no longer have to suffer through sleepless nights or drag yourself through exhausted days. It's possible to start right now sleeping as soundly as a newborn baby—even if you've experienced sleep disorders for all of your life.

Through the power of good sleep hygiene, good nutrition, healthy lifestyle choices, exercise, vitamins, supplements, and, most importantly of all, entering into the peace of God, you can be empowered to sleep soundly and live in the robust health and vigor of a rested life.

Sleep disorders are not your destiny. With God's grace, you will find energy, power, and increasing joy!

Originally published as *The Bible Cure for Sleep Disorders* in 2001, *The New Bible Cure for Sleep Disorders* has been revised and updated with the latest medical research on sleep disorders. If you compare it side by side with the previous edition, you'll see that it's also larger, allowing me to expand greatly upon the information provided in the previous edition and provide you with a deeper understanding of what you face and how to overcome it.

Unchanged from the previous edition are the timeless, life-changing, and healing scriptures throughout this book that will strengthen and encourage your spirit and soul. The proven principles, truths, and guidelines in these passages anchor the practical and medical insights also contained in this book. They will effectively focus your prayers, thoughts, and actions so you can step into God's plan of divine health for you—a plan that includes victory over sleep disorders.

Another change since the original *The Bible Cure for Sleep Disorders* was published is that I've released a foundational book, *The Seven Pillars of Health*. I encourage you to read it because the principles of health it contains are the foundation to healthy living that will affect all areas of your life. It sets the stage for everything you will ever read in any other book I've published—including this one.

It is my prayer that these practical suggestions for health, nutrition, and fitness will bring wholeness to your life—body, soul, and spirit. May they deepen your fellowship with God and strengthen your ability to worship and serve Him.

—DON COLBERT, MD

A **BIBLE CURE** Prayer for You

Dear Lord, I give You all my sleepless nights and exhausted days. You said to come to You for rest, and as I enter the pages of this book, I ask You to help me to find rest in You. Help me to overcome fatigue and become energized to serve and worship You with my whole heart, mind, body, and strength. Empower and strengthen me to find renewal in You for my body, mind, and spirit. In Jesus's name, amen.

REST ASSURED—YOU CAN FIND REST!

ALMIGHTY GOD, WHO created the universe with unparalleled wisdom, also created your body to need rest. As a matter of fact, in His wisdom God made rest a foundational principle for life on Earth. The Bible says, "On the seventh day God had finished his work of creation, so he rested from all his work. And God blessed the seventh day and declared it holy, because it was the day when he rested from his work of creation" (Gen. 2:2–3). Rest is a gift to all the earth's creatures to restore and refresh their physical, mental, and spiritual strength and to renew their vitality.

The rest your body needs is a vital part of living in God's divine health for you, and your loving Creator is committed to seeing that you get it. Take a moment and think about the heavenly Father's heart as you read these words: "The LORD is my shepherd, I shall not want. He makes me lie down in green pastures; He leads me beside quiet waters. He restores my soul" (Ps. 23:1–3, NAS).

If you are suffering because of not getting enough sleep, rest assured. God has provided wisdom to help you to gain a better understanding of the reasons for your fatigue so that you can begin feeling much better very soon.

UNDERSTANDING SLEEP DEPRIVATION

As I mentioned in this book's introduction, I suffered tremendous sleep deprivation during my medical residency and early years of practice. I was on call every fourth night. I often went through the night without sleeping, and then had to work the following day. During that season of my life I felt fatigued and drowsy much of the time.

> When thou liest down, thou shalt not be afraid: yea, thou shalt lie down, and thy sleep shall be sweet.
> —PROVERBS 3:24, KJV

Many professions in today's stressed-out world create fatigue and encourage sleep disorders. It is believed that a century ago, before Thomas Edison invented the light bulb, the average person slept about 10 hours per night. Today, the average individual sleeps 6.9 hours a night.[1] Our modern lifestyles are so full that there's usually not enough time to get everything done, and consequently we tend to short ourselves on sleep. We end up paying for our many activities with drowsiness and fatigue.

Let's take a look at a few statistics related to our growing problem with sleep.

- A 2005 survey by the National Sleep Foundation found 75 percent of adults had at least one symptom of a sleep problem, and 54 percent experienced at least one symptom of insomnia.[2]

- Americans average a little less than seven hours of sleep a night, but sleep experts generally recommend seven to eight hours of sleep a night.[3]

- Approximately 40 percent of adults snore.[4]

- Approximately 60 percent of children, mainly teenagers, report being tired during the day.[5]

- Women suffer from insomnia more often than men.[6]

- As men go from sixteen years of age to fifty years of age, they lose about 80 percent of their deep sleep, according to one study.[7]

- Insomnia is more common in people over the age of sixty-five, with more than half of those over age sixty-five experiencing disturbed sleep.[8]

- Elderly people also commonly take different prescription medications, with insomnia being one of the side effects.[9]

- Elderly people are also more prone to develop anxiety, depression, and grief, which are associated with insomnia.[10]

- Of all adults, 20 to 40 percent have insomnia in the course of a year.[11]

- Over 70 million Americans suffer from disorders of sleep and wakefulness.[12]

- One out of three people have insomnia at some point in their lives.[13]

- Insomnia is the third most frequent health complaint behind headaches (the second) and pain (first).[14]
- People with insomnia are more prone to develop depression.[15]

These statistics are staggering. The less sleep we get, the more we build up our sleep debt, a hard lesson that I learned early in my professional life.

SLEEP DEBT

The health problems I experienced in my thirties were the result of accumulating a huge sleep debt. My body needed a certain amount of sleep per night in order to function at its best. Typically, I need at least eight hours sleep a night in order to function at my best. Instead of getting eight hours of sleep a night during internship and residency, I would only get about one to two hours of sleep at night every fourth night. So, I would have a six- or seven-hour sleep debt on the nights that I was on call.

The difference between the number of hours that you need to sleep each night—which is about eight hours for me—and the number of hours you actually sleep equal your sleep debt. For example, I was sleeping maybe one hour on Monday, eight hours on Tuesday, eight hours on Wednesday, eight hours on Thursday, and one on Friday. Thus I built up a sleep debt of fourteen hours in just five days.

Now, the greater your sleep debt is, the stronger the drive for sleep. Also, your sleep debt is cumulative. A sleep debt is very similar to someone who regularly withdraws more money from their bank account than they deposit. They get further and further into the red as each day passes.

My son recently just graduated from Oral Roberts University, and his last semester was quite difficult. He pulled many all-nighters studying and had accumulated a hefty sleep debt as a result. Also, his first baby was born during the middle of all of this. When my son returned home from school, he slept about twelve to fourteen hours a night for the first couple of weeks after arriving. I understood this as he was repaying his sleep debt that he owed his body.

As you accumulate more and more sleep debt, fatigue and irritability increase, and job performance, memory, and concentration decrease. You are also at a higher risk of having a traffic accident or job injury, and eventually, health problems begin to occur.

Dangers of Too Little Sleep

Sleep needs vary from person to person; however, most sleep experts recommend that adults get seven to eight hours of restful sleep per night; people who practice this tend to be the healthiest. However, as I stated earlier, before Mr. Edison invented the light bulb in 1879, Americans slept an average of ten hours a night. Now, the average American sleeps only 6.9 hours a night.[16] The amount of sleep that you need will typically vary over the course of your life and is dependent on your age, activity level, stress level, health, as well as lifestyle habits. During times of illness or stress, you may typically feel an increased need for sleep. Unfortunately, for most Americans, when they are pressed for time or are working to meet a deadline, the first thing they usually cut back on is sleep. One thing you need to realize is that adequate sleep is not an option or a luxury but a major pillar of good health.

Here's what you risk if you don't get enough rest:

- Increased risk of heart disease. A 2004 study found that women who averaged only five hours of sleep a night were 39 percent more likely to develop heart disease than those who slept eight hours a night.[17]

- Loss of focus, concentration, memory, and creativity, as well as alertness and work performance; problems making decisons

- Less opportunity to recharge, restore, and refresh your brain and body

- Aging more rapidly. Growth hormone is mainly secreted at night as we sleep, along with other hormones that help to keep us looking younger.

- Imbalanced neurotransmitters such as serotonin, norepinephrine, and dopamine, which are commonly associated with anxiety, depression, irritability, grumpiness, and mood swings

- Higher risk of being in auto accidents; approximately one hundred thousand motor vehicle accidents each year are caused by drivers falling asleep at the wheel, causing approximately fifteen thousand deaths per year.[18]

- Compromised immune system and decreased number of natural killer cells resulting in more colds, flu, and other infections. Natural killer cells help prevent cancer as well as infections.

- Increased risk of cancer due to lower natural killer-cell count and a weaker immune system

- Greater risk of obesity. One study found that people who limited their sleep to only four hours a night for several nights experienced changes in hormones that control appetite, resulting in overeating and weight gain.[19]

- Higher risk of type 2 diabetes

- Higher risk of inflammation, which is at the root of most degenerative diseases—including heart disease, cancer, Alzheimer's disease, arthritis, asthma, and many more diseases

- Increased headaches, sore joints, and stomach ailments

Now you've heard about all the medical consequences of too little sleep, but realize there are also medical consequences to sleeping too much.

DANGERS OF TOO MUCH SLEEP

Just as inadequate sleep is associated with many health problems, too much sleep is also associated with its own set of heath issues. Numerous medical problems are associated with too much sleep, including type 2 diabetes and obesity. In one study of almost nine thousand Americans, people who slept over nine hours per night had a 50 percent greater risk of diabetes than individuals who slept seven hours per night. An increased risk of diabetes was also seen in those who slept less than five hours per night.[20]

Also, another study showed that individuals who slept for nine or more hours per night were 21 percent more likely to become obese over a six-year period than those who slept between seven and eight hours per night.[21]

Multiple studies have found that those who sleep nine or more hours per night have a significantly higher death rate than those sleeping seven to eight hours a night.[22]

Researchers have found that in postmenopausal women, those who slept nine or more hours per night were 70 percent more likely to suffer an ischemic stroke than those females who slept an average of seven hours per night. The females who slept six hours or less per night are at a 14 percent higher risk of stroke compared to those who slept seven hours per night.[23]

However, for those sleeping nine hours a night, they should not think that they are going to die early. The best way to determine whether you get enough sleep is by asking yourself two questions:

1. Do you awaken refreshed?
2. Are you alert during the day?

First, you simply must understand that both inadequate sleep as well as too much sleep can be dangerous to your health. You will discover in this book how to recharge your brain and body by learning behavioral therapy methods, sleep hygiene, and developing good health habits as well as taking certain natural supplements. I strongly recommend that you read my book *The Seven Pillars of Health*, which forms a very strong foundation for developing good lifestyle and nutritional habits for health.

SLEEP REQUIREMENTS DURING THE STAGES OF LIFE

As I've stated, most adults require seven to eight hours of sleep a night; however, we did not start off that way. As newborns, we slept approximately twelve to eighteen hours a day and did not adhere to a schedule. However, by six months of age, most infants are able to sleep through the night for about nine to twelve hours and usually take a nap in the morning and afternoon for thirty minutes to two hours.

Toddlers, ages one to three years of age, sleep approximately twelve to fourteen hours a night with just one nap during the day for approximately one to three hours.

Preschoolers, ages three to five, sleep about eleven to thirteen hours a night, and naps are usually shorter. After age five, most children no longer need a nap.

Children six years of age to puberty usually sleep about ten to eleven hours a night. Their sleep patterns are very similar to the sleep pattern of adults.

Adolescents usually need about nine to ten hours of sleep per night, but they usually do not attain it and begin to develop a sleep debt.

After age sixty, most adults still need seven to eight hours sleep a night in order to be refreshed and alert. However, most elderly people have problems getting adequate sleep at night. Elderly individuals need to realize that their overall health is directly associated with good sleep quality as well as an adequate amount of sleep.

SLEEP ARCHITECTURE

To gain an understanding of sleep disorders, it's critically important to understand the stages of sleep. There are two main components of sleep:

- **Non–rapid eye movement (NREM) sleep:**
  NREM is a cycle with four stages: stage one,
  stage two, stage three, and stage four, with stage
  four being the deepest sleep. When you close
  your eyes and doze off, stage one begins.
- **Rapid eye movement (REM) sleep:** By the time
  you've entered stage five, you move into REM
  sleep. This is the level of sleep where dreaming
  takes place. During REM sleep, the brain is very
  active.

Completing a sleep cycle means that you've drifted from being in superficial stage one sleep all the way through stages two and three, and then you entered stage four, your deepest sleep. After that, you entered stage five, which is the dream stage. Here is what happens in each stage:

- **Stage one sleep** is simply the drowsy stage in
  which you drift in and out of being awake.
  During stage one sleep it's easy to be awak-

ened, for you are actually just dozing or are half-awake.

- **Stage two sleep**, on the other hand, is a light level of sleep. Here your heart rate, respiratory rate, and metabolic rate decrease. During stage two you can still be awakened easily.

- **Stage three sleep** is the level where your breathing slows down. Your heart rate slows even more, and your muscles become more relaxed. During this stage the body is able to regenerate, restore, and repair organs and tissues due to the release of growth hormone. You generally reach stage three sleep within thirty minutes of falling asleep. It's more difficult to awaken someone from stage three sleep. When you do wake them up, they tend to be a little groggy.

> I will both lay me down in peace, and sleep: for thou, LORD, only makest me dwell in safety.
> —PSALM 4:8, KJV

- **Stage four sleep** is the deepest level of sleep, and it is the most restorative and refreshing stage of sleep. This stage is reached approximately an hour after falling asleep, and it is by far the most important stage of sleep. After two to three sleep cycles, both stage three and stage four sleep may disappear for the remainder of the night. That's why it's critically important to get uninterrupted, peaceful, restorative sleep for the first three sleep cycles, which occur during the first four and a half hours of sleep. This is the best way to reap the benefit of this deep, restoring, and repairing stage three and stage four sleep.

- **Stage five sleep**—the final stage—is REM sleep, also called dream sleep. During REM sleep the brain is much more active as the brain reacts to your dreams. In fact, the EEG tracing during REM sleep reveals rapid alpha waves that are very similar to the brain waves present when you are awake. Your heart rate and respiratory rate may speed up a little during REM sleep.

SLEEP DIARY

Making sure your body benefits from all the stages of sleep can be a challenge, as we have seen earlier with so many Americans getting so little sleep each night, but you do not have to be one of the statistics. I recommend keeping a sleep diary because it will enable you to make some key observations in order to determine your true sleep problem. Complete your sleep diary each morning upon waking. If you are taking sleep aids, please refrain from taking them while you are keeping this sleep diary so that you can know the pure details of your sleep issue. Please be sure to include the following information in your diary:

1. The time you went to bed and the time you woke up

2. How long it took you to fall asleep

3. The times you woke up during the night and how long it took you to fall back asleep

4. How much caffeine you consumed during the day and the time that you consumed it

5. Anything you ate as a meal or snack in the evening and the time you ate it

6. Any naps you took

7. Any medications you took

8. Rating of the quality of your sleep in terms of restful with no awakenings, to few awakenings, frequent awakenings, awakened but fell back to sleep, and finally, awakened and stayed awake

9. Your level of mental alertness when you woke up in the morning (Were you groggy or refreshed?)

10. Any physical, emotional, or environmental factors that disturbed your sleep (a snoring spouse, a hot room, television noise, traffic noise, a storm, attending to the needs of a child, stress, recurrent preoccupations, worrisome thoughts, heartburn, coughing, illness, and so on)

It is best to keep a sleep diary for two to four weeks continuously; date each day. When you awaken in the morning (not in the middle of the night), simply write down your observations before you get out of bed.

Hosea 4:6 says, "My people are destroyed for lack of knowledge" (NKJV). By filling out your sleep diary, you will probably be able to discover the particular sleep disorder you have.

This book will show you how you can most likely correct that problem.

CONCLUSION

Lying awake in the middle of the night trying to doze off can seem more miserable than nearly anything else. Still, your rest is very important to God, for it is a key principle of all that He created. God desires that you enjoy blessed rest.

His wonderful Word says, "It is vain for you to rise up early, to sit up late, to eat the bread of sorrows; for so He gives His beloved sleep" (Ps. 127:2, NKJV).

God promises to bless you with the gift of sleep. I believe that with sound wisdom and God's help, you are beginning to put those endless nights of sleeplessness behind you!

A BIBLE CURE Prayer for You

Dear Lord, I thank You that You have provided for my sleep. If my way of living is breaking any of Your principles of health and sound wisdom, I ask You to reveal it to me. Let my life line up in every way with Your perfect will so that I can enjoy the full benefits of Your blessed sleep. Amen.

A **BIBLE CURE** *Prescription*

Take time to contemplate the factors that may contribute to your sleeplessness. For example, do you wait until the last minute to prepare yourself for the next day? Are you one who just has to catch a late-night movie or the evening news? Do you sacrifice sleep to finish a project just in time for a deadline? Do you just have to have a late-night snack or a few glasses of wine before bed? Think carefully about how your habits may affect your sleep quality, and make a list here of what you may be doing to hinder a good night's sleep. Return to this list with solutions as you continue through this Bible Cure book.

_____

_____

_____

_____

_____

_____

REST ASSURED BY BEING INFORMED ABOUT SLEEP DISORDERS

THERE ARE TWO main categories into which sleep disorders fall:

1. Dyssomnias—characterized by problems with either falling asleep or staying asleep, followed by excessive drowsiness during the day. Examples of dyssomnias include insomnia, sleep apnea, narcolepsy, restless legs syndrome, periodic limb movements, and advanced and delayed sleep phase syndrome.

2. Parasomnias—abnormalities in behavior that occur during sleep, such as night terrors (a frightening activity during sleep), nightmares, sleepwalking and/or sleep talking, bruxism (or grinding your teeth), sleep-related eating disorder, and REM sleep behavior disorder

Let's investigate some of these extremely unpleasant sleeping problems.

THE NIGHTMARE OF INSOMNIA

Insomnia is by far the most common sleep disorder. It is characterized by having problems either falling asleep or staying asleep. There are two main forms of insomnia: primary insomnia and secondary insomnia.

Primary insomnia

Primary insomnia is not due to medical, psychiatric, or environmental problems, nor is it due to medications or any other substances. The insomnia is its own disorder, which means the insomnia is the medical condition and not a symptom of some other medical or psychiatric disease.

Usually primary insomnia is a lone disorder that develops over time. Studies have shown that people with chronic insomnia produce higher levels of stress hormones than other people. Since primary insomnia is its own disorder and is usually associated with stress, I strongly recommend that you read my book *Stress Less*. Using behavioral techniques, sleep hygiene techniques, relaxation techniques, and nutritional supplements will generally help to reverse primary insomnia. These methods will be discussed in detail later in this book.

Secondary insomnia

The most common type of insomnia, secondary insomnia is a symptom or side effect of some other medical or emotional problem such as anxiety, depression, chronic pain, heart failure, asthma, acid reflux, menopause with hot flashes and night sweats, urological disorders, and so forth. Secondary insomnia can also be due to a side effect of certain medications, especially cold and sinus medications, asthma medications, and more.

Secondary insomnia may also be due to caffeine, nicotine, or alcohol.

It is believed that more than eight out of ten people with insomnia suffer from secondary insomnia. Since over 80 percent of patients with insomnia have secondary insomnia, it is critically important to treat the primary problem.[1]

For example, if your insomnia is due to an enlarged prostate and you have to get up multiple times during the night to urinate, simply treating the enlarged prostate will generally correct the insomnia. Also, if your insomnia is due to hot flashes or acid reflux, simply treating the hot flashes or acid reflux will generally get rid of the insomnia. If your insomnia is due to anxiety or depression, then simply treating the anxiety and depression will usually take care of the insomnia.

The good news is that controlling secondary insomnia is fairly easy. Usually this is accomplished by simply treating the primary problem, employing a few behavioral techniques, and following a regimen of sleep hygiene and a few natural supplements. I will cover all of these steps for managing insomnia in the remaining chapters of this book.

SLEEP APNEA

Sleep apnea affects over 18 million Americans, and approximately 10 million Americans are not even diagnosed. Over 50 percent of all the patients with sleep apnea are over forty years of age. Sleep apnea is more common in men than women, with 4–9 percent of middle-aged men with apnea and only 2–4 percent of middle-aged women with apnea.[2]

After menopause, women lose the protective effect of estrogen and progesterone, and the risk of developing obstructive sleep apnea increases significantly, nearly to the rate seen in men. African Americans have a higher risk of sleep apnea than any other ethnic group.

Sleep apnea may eventually lead to hypertension, arrhythmias, congestive heart failure, stroke, coronary artery disease, heart attacks, cardiac arrest, pulmonary hypertension, type 2 diabetes, memory loss, and depression. One study found that one's risk of stroke doubles over a seven-year period if one has sleep apnea.[3]

Sleep apnea is believed to have contributed to the death of football Hall of Famer Reggie White.[4] Sleep apnea is also associated with severe fatigue and daytime sleepiness, memory loss, irritability, accidents, and premature death. How does one differentiate snoring from the potentially deadly sleep apnea? Well, first of all, the symptoms are usually different with sleep apnea.

Symptoms

A patient with sleep apnea usually has severely loud snoring, which is usually interrupted with extended times of silence followed by a gasping, choking, or snorting sound.

People who sleep alone are many times not even aware that they snore or stop breathing, but they usually have specific signs and symptoms of sleep apnea that can still be recognized.

These patients usually have a large neck. Men with sleep apnea usually have a neck circumference greater than 17 inches, and many times much larger than this. Females usually have a neck circumference greater than 16 inches.

They also usually have extreme daytime sleepiness and tend to fall asleep whenever they get quiet for a few minutes, such as at the movies or sitting at one's desk after eating lunch or even during a business meeting. They also commonly feel spacey or like they are in a fog.

Gaining weight also increases a person's risk of developing sleep apnea; conversely, sleep apnea increases their risk of gaining even more weight! This is primarily because people with sleep apnea are usually too tired to do any type of exercise.

People with sleep apnea also usually have problems with concentration, memory, reaction time, and learning. Their brains have been deprived of oxygen, and they are usually simply exhausted from the lack of quality sleep.

Continued oxygen deprivation places a strain on the heart and lungs and eventually may raise the blood pressure as the vital organs are literally being starved of oxygen. This is why people with sleep apnea have an increased risk of hypertension, heart problems (including heart attacks and cardiac arrest), type 2 diabetes, and even depression.

Family history of sleep apnea typically increases a person's risk of sleep apnea two to four times.

During a sleep apnea episode, breathing can stop for about ten seconds to as long as a minute. You then wake up to breathe, and typically awaken gasping for air. This cycle of waking up to breathe can occur hundreds of times a night.

There are three kinds of sleep apnea: obstructive sleep apnea, central sleep apnea, and mixed sleep apnea.

Obstructive sleep apnea

Obstructive sleep apnea is the most common type of this very serious disorder, occurring in about 2 to 4 percent of all middle-aged adults.[5] Most people with sleep apnea don't even realize they suffer from it!

> The sleep of the working man is pleasant, whether he eats little or much; but the full stomach of the rich man does not allow him to sleep.
> —ECCLESIASTES 5:12, NAS

In this condition the upper airway becomes completely obstructed for ten seconds or longer. During these episodes, blood levels of oxygen decrease and carbon dioxide levels increase.

It's this change in the blood gases that alerts the sleeper's brain that the lungs need to start breathing again. But for this to occur, the brain must awaken the body from sleep. These apneic episodes may occur twenty to hundreds of times a night, awaking the sleeper each time—although he may not realize it. As you can imagine, the result is daytime drowsiness, depression, and learning and memory problems.

More than half of the individuals who have sleep apnea are overweight.[6] In addition, if a man or woman has a large neck, a double chin, and truncal obesity (obesity around the abdominal region), there seems to be an increased correlation with obstructive sleep apnea also. The larger the neck size and the more alcohol that is consumed, the higher the correlation with this sleep disorder.[7]

In order to diagnose sleep apnea, you need to undergo a sleep study at a sleep lab. A sleep study usually measures oxygen saturation, episodes of apnea, body movements, body temperature, pulse, respiration, eye movement, and brain activity. All sleep labs allow sleep in a comfortable environment.

Sleep apnea is usually treated with CPAP (continuous positive airway pressure) or BiPAP (bilevel positive airway pressure). AVAPS (average volume assured pressure support) is a new technology in treating sleep apnea introduced into the United States in 2007. It ensures an adequate depth of breathing and is a special feature to some special BiPAP machines. Also, newer models of CPAP machines are quieter and lighter and have many options and a variety of mask styles.

Years ago, some of my patients on CPAP machines would literally jerk their mask off their face in the middle of the night and throw them across the room. Now there are new, very comfortable models that fit the face and nose well. Weight loss and especially decreasing your neck size are often useful in relieving or decreasing the severity of sleep apnea. Somnoplasty may also benefit those with mild sleep apnea. This is discussed under snoring.

As you lose weight, be sure that you exercise, which usually helps to decrease your neck size. Additional information on this subject can be found in my books *The Seven Pillars of Health* and *The Bible Cure for Weight Loss and Muscle Gain*.

Central sleep apnea

Central sleep apnea occurs when the brain's respiratory centers do not send a message to start breathing. This type of sleep apnea is common in those with congestive heart failure, chronic obstructive pulmonary disease (COPD), as well as neurologic diseases. Therapy is typically aimed at treating the underlying medical problems such as congestive heart failure.

Mixed sleep apnea

Mixed sleep apnea is a combination of obstructive sleep apnea and central sleep apnea, but it is also a result of an obstructed airway.

DOES YOUR PARTNER'S SNORING KEEP YOU AWAKE?

Does your partner happily saw logs all night while you watch the ceiling? If your spouse snores, it could be sign of sleep apnea. But remember that even though all patients with sleep apnea snore, all snorers do not have sleep apnea. Have your partner undergo a medical evaluation if he or she seems to stop breathing for short periods of time.

Snoring that is not related to sleep apnea does not pose any health risks and does not cause daytime drowsiness for the snorer. However, it does for the snorer's spouse. Snoring is also fairly difficult to cure.

> Indeed, he who watches over Israel never slumbers or sleeps.
>
> —PSALM 121:4

Snoring is one of the most common sleep problems in the United States, affecting about 42 percent of men and 31 percent of women.[8] Those who snore often have anatomical differences such as an obstructed nasal passage, a deviated nasal septum, or an elongation of the uvula (which is the tissue that hangs down the back of the throat), or the snoring may be due to sagging of the soft palate. Enlarged tonsils or adenoids can cause snoring also, as well as poor muscle tone in the tissues of the soft palate, throat, and tongue.

Gaining weight usually increases snoring simply because the body eventually deposits the extra fat in the lining of the throat, causing the breathing passages to narrow more and more. Also, the uvula actually elongates as we age and gain weight.

If your spouse is an overweight snorer, losing weight and exercising is the best advice for him or her—a weight loss of just 10 to 15 pounds can make a big difference!

Changing sleeping positions can also help. Try sewing a pocket into the back of a T-shirt and placing a tennis ball or a plastic ball in it to keep your happy snorer from sleeping on his back.

If your spouse's weight or sleeping position is not the issue, there may be other common triggers of snoring. Is it nasal congestion, a deviated nasal septum, enlarged tonsils or adenoids, or decreased muscle tone in the throat with a sagging uvula or soft palate? Or it is alcohol or medication?

For nasal congestion, I generally recommend a homeopathic herbal over-the-counter decongestant, which generally helps. Breathe Right strips, a decongestant, or a nasal steroid such as Flonase or Nasonex will help to open the nasal passages and may prevent snoring. Your spouse may also benefit from using a humidifier or snoring sprays, which simply lubricate the back of the throat with some type of oil such as olive oil, almond oil, or grape seed oil. These oils help prevent the soft tissues from sticking together.

Other things to do include avoiding alcohol, muscle relaxants, tranquilizers, and sleep medications since they tend to relax the muscles of the throat, which can worsen snoring. Cigarette smoke can also cause the tissues of the throat to swell and thus encourage snoring.

Many snorers have a sagging uvula or soft palate. Dental devices are reported to help many snorers. There are more than fifty different variations available. These are usually either a mandibular advancing device, which advances the lower jaw, or a tongue-retaining device that holds the tongue forward. These devices are usually purchased from dentists who are specifically trained in treating patients who snore. Or you can also purchase a snore alarm at specialty stores. A snore alarm is simply a wristwatch that vibrates as soon a person begins to snore.

When severe snoring persists even after trying the above techniques, especially in the case of a deviated septum or enlarged adenoids, some consider surgery. However, for a sagging soft palate or uvula, I would first recommend trying somnoplasty before considering surgery. Somnoplasty uses radiofrequency ablation to simply shrink the soft tissues of the soft palate. It is performed as an outpatient procedure under local anesthesia. A tiny probe sends out radio waves that shrink the tissues. There is minimal pain with or after the procedure and minimal post-op complications. It may need to be repeated to achieve the best results.

For a nonsnoring spouse, try a background noise machine (which can be purchased at Brookstone). The sound of a waterfall, raindrops, or white noise can usually drown out a snoring spouse. You might also get some soft earplugs until your snoring partner has been treated, or, if none of the above measures help, consider sleeping in another bedroom.

NARCOLEPSY

Narcolepsy is rare and affects as many as two hundred thousand Americans, and as many as 12 percent have a close relative with the disease.[9] Narcolepsy is a neurological sleep disorder where the brain does not properly regulate the daily cycle of sleep and wakefulness. In other words, the brain is unable to regulate the sleep/wake cycles normally, and the patients suffer from REM sleep abnormality.

Patients with narcolepsy become drowsy during the day and may fall asleep at an inappropriate time, such as during an important business meeting. They also may experience sleep paralysis, cataplexy, hallucinations, and insomnia. Cataplexy is a sudden loss of muscle function while awake, is usually brief, and occurs in approximately 70 percent of patients with narcolepsy.[10] This may occur with any strong emotion, including anger or laughter. In severe cases, the muscles become paralyzed and the person may drop to the floor. About 50 percent of patients with narcolepsy also suffer from sleep paralysis. They are typically unable to move or talk for a few minutes when they are falling asleep or when they are waking up.[11] Also, approximately 50 percent experience hallucinations, which may be frightening sounds, feelings, or images from dreams as they are falling asleep or waking up.[12]

If an individual has severe sleepiness during the day and cataplexy, he or she most likely has narcolepsy. These patients should have a sleep study in order to diagnose narcolepsy. I find that most of these patients also have severe adrenal fatigue. Many patients with narcolepsy will also need a medication such as Provigil, which promotes wakefulness and has few side effects.

Again, a regular bedtime schedule, sleep hygiene, stress reduction techniques, and relaxation techniques may help many with narcolepsy. Support groups are also important for those with narcolepsy. Supplements to help adrenal fatigue are found in my book *Stress Less*.

INSOMNIA AND MOVEMENT DISORDERS

There are two movement disorders that frequently cause insomnia: restless legs syndrome and periodic limb movement disorder. These movement disorders are actually neurological sleep disorders. Restless legs syndrome usually keeps a person awake, whereas periodic limb movement disorder usually keeps a person's *spouse* awake. Let's look at each disorder.

Restless legs syndrome (RLS)

Restless legs syndrome affects as many as 12 million Americans.[13] It is a neurological sleep disorder that is characterized by an urge to move the legs, strange feelings in the legs (especially the calves), crawling sensations (like worms crawling on the skin) in the legs, as well as pulling sensations, tingling, and prickling sensations.

These sensations usually start in the evening, but they also may occur in the daytime as a person sits at a desk, watches TV, or even plays. The sensations usually worsen when a person lies down for sleep.

Simply moving your legs or pacing, massaging, or stretching your legs usually relieves the discomfort temporarily; it also helps you cope temporarily. But since these sensations usually occur at night when lying in bed, they can seriously interfere with sleep, causing you to get in and out of bed repeatedly during the night. Over time, you will become exhausted and more prone to develop depression.

The cause of RLS is unknown, but it is believed to be a glitch in the neurological pathways through which the brain controls movement and is believed to involve the neurotransmitter dopamine. This disorder does run in families, and a child of a patient with RLS has a 50 percent risk of inheriting it.[14]

Restless legs syndrome is also associated with other medical conditions, including iron-deficiency anemia, diabetes, kidney failure, neuropathy, arthritis, and Parkinson's disease. Also, certain medications can make it worse, including lithium, antihistamines, and antidepressants. Excessive caffeine, nicotine, and stress can also worsen it.

RLS is more common after age fifty.[15] Moderate aerobic exercise such as cycling or walking usually helps to decrease symptoms, whereas excessive exercise may worsen symptoms. Taking a warm bath with 1–4 cups of Epsom salts (hydrated magnesium sulfate) added to your bathwater may also help decrease symptoms.

If you have RLS, your doctor should run blood tests to check for anemia. You should also have your iron, ferritin, and magnesium levels checked. In addition, I recommend that your doctor check for diabetes or kidney problems.

Iron and magnesium supplements may help you with restless legs syndrome, but only take iron supplements if your blood test shows that you are anemic and have low iron levels.

Most men and postmenopausal women should not need iron supplements; if they are anemic, it may be due to a slow GI bleed, colon cancer, ulcer, gastritis, hemorrhoids, or acid reflux.

You need to be evaluated by a primary care physician and usually a GI specialist if this is the case.

I also recommend cutting back on caffeine and stopping nicotine as well as alcohol. Stretching exercises, relaxation yoga, massaging the legs, and using heating pads often help to relieve RLS. I always place patients with RLS on a comprehensive multivitamin with a chelated magnesium supplement and a fish oil supplement. This may provide significant relief within a few weeks.

If your restless legs syndrome is very severe and affecting your sleep significantly, talk to your doctor about a medication called Requip, which usually provides significant relief. This medication is very helpful and approved for treating RLS; it is also used to treat Parkinson's disease.

Periodic limb movement disorder (PLMD)

Periodic limb movement disorder is associated with involuntary contractions and movements of the legs and occasionally the arms while one is sleeping. These movements of the legs are typically jerking or kicking movements that last about thirty seconds and may occur hundreds of times a night.

It is different from restless legs syndrome, which occurs when one is awake and the movements are voluntary. PLMD, on the other hand, occurs while one is asleep and the movements are involuntary.

Many patients with PLMD are not even aware that their legs jerk in their sleep. However, their spouse is usually very aware. Usually, the spouse is the one being awakened many times during the night and is the one suffering from insomnia, not the offender.

This neurological sleep disorder is also probably related to the neurotransmitter dopamine and is more common in elderly individuals. I treat this disorder similar to RLS and run the same blood tests as RLS. I also put patients with PLMD on a comprehensive multivitamin, chelated magnesium, and fish oil. If their condition is severe, they will also usually benefit from the medication Requip.

CIRCADIAN RHYTHMS

Everyone has a twenty-four-hour internal clock, also called a biological clock, that is regulated by the brain's master clock in the hypothalamus of the brain. This area of the hypothalamus is called the suprachiasmatic nucleus, or SCN. Everyone has their own individualized circadian rhythm or natural sleep/wake cycles. These help to regulate numerous important biological activities such as waking up, sleeping, the release of certain hormones (including melatonin and cortisol), blood pressure, body temperature, blood sugar levels, digestive secretions, and so on.

Our brains are actually programmed for activity during the daylight and are programmed to sleep when it gets dark, based upon our circadian rhythms. Before electricity was developed, almost everyone went to bed when it was dark and awakened whenever it was light outside. Now, however, with the help of bright lights, TVs, computer screens, and more, many have confused their brains into thinking that it is daytime when in reality it is the middle of the night. Also, nightclubs, late-night shopping and dining, late-night movies, the Internet, shift work, and artificial lighting have disrupted many people's circadian rhythms or natural sleep/wake cycles. Many have developed insomnia as a result of this.

One's biological clock responds to several external cues, which help to keep it set on a twenty-four-hour schedule. These cues are called zeitgebers and include light and melatonin. However, light is the most significant cue.

PROBLEMS WITHIN CIRCADIAN RHYTHMS

In order for you to perform at your best, your circadian rhythms or natural sleep/wake cycles need to be synchronized with your work and lifestyle.

In the United States, the majority of Americans go to work at 8:00 or 9:00 a.m. and then work until 5:00 or 6:00 p.m. In order to work those hours and get eight hours of sleep at night, most people should go to bed at 10:00 or 11:00 p.m. and wake up at 6:00 or 7:00 a.m. Now, if you have a one- to two-hour commute to work, you will need to go to bed even earlier and wake up earlier. However, people whose internal biological clock is out of sync typically cannot go to sleep when they need to go to sleep and suffer the consequences as a result.

Night owls

Night owls are those individuals with delayed sleep phase syndrome (DSPS). They generally stay up late at night and usually do not fall asleep until 2:00 or 3:00 a.m.—or sometimes even later. They then enjoy sleeping until late morning or early afternoon. This is very common with students in high school and college.

The problem for night owls is that most jobs require you to be at work at 8:00 or 9:00 a.m. unless you are lucky enough to find a good job that starts around 2:00 or 3:00 in the afternoon. Good luck with that. Otherwise, you need to adjust your circadian rhythm accordingly. Many musicians and artists have delayed sleep phase syndrome and do not even realize it. Treatment for delayed sleep phase syndrome for night owls includes chronotherapy, light therapy, and melatonin.

Chronotherapy simply delays sleep in two- or three-hour increments daily until the patient's sleeping and waking patterns are normalized. It is fairly difficult to do, and I rarely use it. The patient must closely adhere to this new schedule. For example, with a patient, who typically falls asleep at 3:00 a.m. but desires to fall asleep at 11:00 p.m., we would first move his bedtime up to 6:00 a.m. on Friday night, then to 9:00 a.m. on Saturday morning, 12 noon on Sunday, 3:00 p.m. on Monday, 6:00 p.m. on Tuesday, 9:00 p.m. on Wednesday, and finally move it to 11:00 p.m. on Thursday.

Now, in an order to do this, I may also need to give a temporary sleeping pill such as Ambien or Rozerem. Rozerem helps to shift the circadian rhythms. Also, one or more of the supplements discussed in chapter 6 may be in order to help the patient fall asleep. One also needs to practice sleep hygiene, relaxation techniques, and stress-reduction techniques.

Light therapy, which will be discussed with other therapies in chapter 5, can also treat delayed sleep phase syndrome. Patients with DSPS may also improve with melatonin a few hours before bedtime as the lights are dimmed. I usually recommend 3–6 mg of melatonin dissolved in the mouth.

Early birds

Early birds are patients who have advanced sleep phase syndrome (ASPS) and are the exact opposite of patients with delayed sleep phase syndrome. These individuals usually start getting sleepy around 7:00 or 8:00 p.m. and then awaken between 3:00 and 5:00 a.m. They usually have no trouble falling asleep, have normal sleep architecture, and are not sleepy during the day. However, they usually think they have insomnia because they awaken typically between 3:00 and 5:00 a.m. and simply cannot fall back to sleep. They may lead very boring social lives since they are usually asleep by 8:00 p.m.

This disorder is also treated with light therapy and melatonin. However, early birds do not respond well to chronotherapy. These individuals typically benefit from wearing a light visor or sitting in a light box between 7:00 and 9:00 p.m., which delays their circadian rhythm. Their bedroom must be totally dark; I recommend blackout curtains and covering every little light with black electrical tape. I may treat patients with ASPS with 1 mg of melatonin in the morning to delay the circadian rhythm and a larger dose of 3–6 mg of melatonin at bedtime. It should be taken around 9:00 or 10:00 p.m.

Jet lag

The main symptom of jet lag is severe fatigue. Typically, people flying north and south do not experience jet lag since they do not cross any time zones. Individuals traveling east usually experience the worst jet lags since they lose an hour for every time zone they cross. Typically, the brain can adjust its biological clock by an hour or two each day; however, three or more hours is a different story. When you fly from Atlanta to

London, you cross five time zones, and even though the local time in London is 9:00 a.m., your body's internal clock still thinks it is 4:00 a.m. Your brain is getting conflicting messages as the sunlight tells your brain to wake up, but your internal clock and lack of sleep are telling you to sleep.

Jet lag affects everyone, but there are ways you can minimize these effects. First, start two or three days before a trip when you are crossing three or four time zones by adjusting your watch and clock to the new time zone. Then try to go to bed at the time you normally go to bed, but do so on the new time zone schedule that your watch is now set to. You may want to start the process a few days earlier if you have to cross four or more time zones. I also strongly recommend 3–6 mg of melatonin that is dissolved in the mouth at bedtime and that you maintain good sleep hygiene.

Shift work

Unfortunately, most workers doing shift work live in constant disruption of the circadian rhythms. Long-term shift work increases the risk of heart disease. One study found a modest increased risk of breast cancer in long-term employees who work night shift when compared to those who did not.[16]

These individuals need to practice good sleep hygiene and avoid morning sunlight by trying to get home and in bed as soon as possible, preferably before sunrise. Try to minimize exposure to sunlight by wearing dark sunglasses on your drive home that cover the sides and tops of your eyes, preventing sunlight shining in. Make your bedroom as dark as possible with blackout curtains, and soundproof your bedroom to keep daytime noise out. Turn off the phone in your bedroom. Also, it is good to take a twenty-minute power nap once a day if you become fatigued. I also recommend taking 3–6 mg of melatonin dissolved in the mouth at bedtime.

Artificial light pollution

The sky glow of Los Angeles is visible from an airplane approximately two hundred miles away; this is also true of many other cities.[17] Sky glow is simply one form of light pollution. The International Agency for Research on Cancer has classified light at night as a group IIA carcinogen (a probable carcinogen).[18] Light at night inhibits the nighttime increase of melatonin, which is the hormone that also has oncostatic properties (tumor-prevention properties).

Artificial light also disrupts our circadian rhythms. Whenever light shines on your eyes or even your skin, it stimulates the release of cortisol—the stress hormone that causes your brain to think it is morning. Many people have numerous little lights in their bedroom from their alarm clock, phone, TV components, alarm system, and so on. These artificial lights may be keeping you from a good night's sleep.

The worst type of artificial light at night is green, blue, and white lights. Candlelight, orange, or red light is not nearly as harmful, so when purchasing an alarm clock, do not choose one with a green or blue light, but rather purchase one with a red light. Also, it is important to cover the alarm clock with a hand towel in order to prevent any light from shining on your eyes or even your skin.

There is epidemiological evidence that shows that the incidence of cancer increases in people living in environments where light pollution is high. In animal studies, destruction of the biological clock actually accelerates experimental cancer growth.[19] It is important for us to realize that artificial light is a probable carcinogen. We should then cover all artificial light in our bedrooms and make sure that we have blackout curtains in order to prevent artificial light from streetlights and sky glows from affecting our sleep.

PARASOMNIAS

Parasomnias are simply sleep disorders that cause strange behaviors while one is asleep. Let us look at some of the most common parasomnias.

Night terrors

Night terrors are entirely different from nightmares. In night terrors, the sleeper usually has no memory or little memory of the episode. He or she usually awakens disoriented and confused and typically experiences increased pulse, increased blood pressure, sweating, rapid breathing, extreme agitation, and dilated pupils.

The sleeper also usually sits up in bed, terrified, and screams a terrifying scream. He then may gasp, moan, or thrash on the bed. Sometimes sleepwalking can accompany night terrors.

This disorder is not associated with dreaming, but it occurs during non-REM sleep; the sleeper is simply caught in between sleep and awakening.

Children tend to suffer more from night terrors than adults, with up to 6 percent of children and less than 1 percent of adults experiencing them.[20] Children typically outgrow them.

When a child or adult experiences a night terror, simply talk to him quietly in a comforting voice. Be careful to touch him

only when he is calming down, since the touch may be misin-
terpreted as an attack.

It is also very important to maintain a regular sleep time to
avoid sleep deprivation. Read your child a lighthearted bedtime
story and not a scary story to help relieve his or her stress and
anxiety. Cognitive-behavioral therapy or counseling may also be
helpful in some individuals. We also use acupressure techniques
that are a combination of applied kinesiology and acupressure
that helps relieve fear, anxiety, and stress, as well as other techniques to help identify and remove any traumatic triggers. Also,
remove caffeinated beverages from the diet, especially in the late
afternoon and evening time.

Nightmares

Nightmares, as opposed to night terrors, occur during REM
sleep, or dream sleep. The sleeper is not confused or disoriented
and recalls the dream. He or she usually does not have the physical symptoms associated with night terrors either.

Nightmares are frightening dreams that are usually related
to a shocking or frightening experience. Certain medications—
including narcotics, antidepressants, and sleep aids—may cause
nightmares as a side effect. Also, alcohol and drug abuse may
be associated with nightmares. Nightmares are common when
one is weaning off or stopping benzodiazepines, such as Xanax
or Valium, or weaning off alcohol or barbiturates. Even certain
foods such as chocolate may cause nightmares. They occur in
up to 7 percent of adults and are more common in children.[21]

However, good sleep hygiene and regular bedtimes are very
important in overcoming nightmares. Refusing to watch any
scary movies or TV shows and even late-night news is also

very important. If nightmares do not improve, we generally recommend cognitive-behavioral therapy and/or counseling. I commonly help patients with nightmares using acupressure techniques in order to remove traumatic triggers.

Sleepwalking

Sleepwalking (somnambulism) is very common in children, with as many as 15 percent of school-age children sleepwalking at least once and approximately 1 percent of adults sleepwalking.[22]

Usually, treatment for sleepwalking is not necessary since most will eventually outgrow it. However, if someone is prone to injure himself through sleepwalking, it is important to organize the bedroom and remove any clutter in order to reduce the chance of falling. Also, it is important to lock all doors and windows in order to confine the sleepwalker to the bedroom. You can put some small wind chimes up in the doorway in order to alert you when the sleepwalker is moving around.

When you encounter the sleepwalker, it is important to gently guide him back to their bed with a gentle, reassuring voice. Do not shake him, yell at him, or try to awaken him. He may misinterpret that as an attack and try to defend himself. Remain calm. The sleepwalker usually responds well to stress-reduction techniques, relaxation techniques, good sleep hygiene, and a regular bedtime schedule. If the sleepwalking continues or worsens, he or she may benefit from cognitive-behavioral therapy or counseling. Some may also benefit from targeted amino acid therapy, which uses amino acids to correct neurotransmitter imbalances. Visit www.NeuroRelief.com for more information.

Sleep-related eating disorder

This disorder affects up to 3 percent of the population. However, a higher percent, up to 15 percent, have an eating disorder. Sleep-related eating disorder typically involves sleepwalking and eating while asleep. Approximately, two-thirds of these patients are female, and approximately half are overweight.[23] They usually consume junk food and sweets but may eat cat food, dog food, or cookie dough. The medications Ambien and lithium may occasionally trigger this disorder. Also, stress, depression, eating disorders, personality disorders, and insomnia may trigger this. However, eliminating the triggering medications and stopping their sleepwalking will usually control the problem. Please follow the instructions for sleepwalking.

Bruxism

Bruxism is simply grinding the teeth. This can ultimately damage and destroy the teeth and also damage the TMJ, which is the temporomandibular joint of the jaw. TMJ disorder is usually associated with severe pain in the jaw and headaches. The pain can also be transferred to the ears or the neck. The severe grinding of the teeth also typically awakens the spouse. Approximately 8 percent of people grind their teeth, and most are not even aware of it.[24]

To correct this problem, I usually refer my patients to a dentist knowledgeable in bruxism and TMJ disorder in order to fit them with a nocturnal bite splint, which protects their teeth and jaw. I also refer them to a cognitive-behavioral therapist and/or counseling as well as teach them stress-reduction techniques and relaxation techniques. They also usually benefit from good sleep hygiene, including a regular bedtime schedule. I will also have them cut down on caffeine and alcohol, especially in the afternoon and evening time. Some of the supplements for insomnia are also beneficial for those patients with bruxism. This will be discussed in chapter 6.

REM sleep behavior disorder

This is a fairly rare parasomnia occurring in only about 0.5 percent of the population; the majority is older men, typically over the age of sixty.[25]

This is a potentially dangerous disorder that can cause harm to the patient or his spouse. It is typically due to a glitch occurring with a mechanism that is supposed to paralyze the body during sleep; as the person dreams, he actually begins to act out his dreams. Occasionally, the dreams are so intense that the person may injure himself or his spouse without even realizing it. The cause is unknown; however, certain medical conditions may precipitate it, including Parkinson's disease, dementia, some brain tumors and masses, and even narcolepsy.[26]

Patients with this disorder need to see a neurologist as well as a primary care physician for a comprehensive physical exam, neurological exam, and typically an MRI of the brain. Guns, knives, sharp objects, and all potentially dangerous objects should be removed from the bedroom. These patients usually need medication in order to control this potentially dangerous disorder. Good sleep hygiene—including a regular bedtime schedule—stress reduction, and relaxation exercises may also be beneficial.

SEE YOUR DOCTOR

If you are experiencing a sleep disorder, it's important that you see your doctor. Get him or her to give you a thorough exam to rule out any serious medical or psychological problem that might be a factor.

CONCLUSION

Sleep disorders plague millions of people every day, the most common offender being insomnia, and while there may not be a cure-all for each one, there is absolutely no reason for you to lose hope that you will ever find rest. Many of these disorders can be treated naturally without drugs. The best thing is that you know what you are facing, because knowing is half the battle. Read on to see the God-given treatments that fulfill His promise of sweet sleep for you.

A **BIBLE CURE** Prayer for You

Thank You, God, for leading me into a path of knowledge, because the footsteps of the righteous are ordered by the Lord. I confess that my sleep is sweet, and I awaken refreshed and renewed. In Jesus's name, amen.

A **BIBLE CURE** *Prescription*

Over the years, I've heard many complaints about sleep problems from my patients. The most common complaints are:

1. Problems falling asleep

2. Problems staying asleep

3. Early morning awakenings

4. Difficulty getting up in the morning

5. Doing unusual things in your sleep

6. Your spouse inadvertently waking you up

7. Inability to stay awake during the day

Do you recognize yourself in any of these descriptions? If you can identify with even one item on this list on an ongoing basis, you are likely dealing with a sleep disorder. But know that God is for you and wants you to be healed. Write a prayer according to Psalm 116:7, thanking Him for that.

_____

_____

_____

_____

_____

REST ASSURED THROUGH PROPER NUTRITION

NOT ONLY DID God create the world to be founded upon a principle of rest, but He also created a dynamic display of delicious fruits, vegetables, and many other foods to provide you with a wonderful array of nutritious choices. All that your body needs for divine health and rest has been bountifully provided for you by your loving heavenly Father. It's no wonder the psalmist declared, "Return to your rest, O my soul, for the LORD has dealt bountifully with you" (Ps. 116:7, NKJV).

Learning how to use God's wisdom in giving your body the right nutritional selections can be a mighty key in breaking the power of sleep disorders and finding rest for your weary body and soul.

Let's take a look at how nutrition can help you.

EATING TO HELP GET YOUR REST

What you eat and what you don't eat are major keys in how well you sleep, for nutrition and sleep are very much related.

Eating a healthy, well-balanced diet is vitally important for getting a good night's sleep. You should get plenty of B-complex vitamins, calcium, magnesium, and other essential nutrients in your diet. Taking a comprehensive multivitamin such as Divine Health Multivitamin will enable you to obtain these nutrients.

In addition, if your diet is made up of fast foods and junk foods, your body may not be getting enough L-tryptophan, which is a powerful amino acid that helps you sleep. Here's how it works. L-tryptophan is the amino acid that is the precursor to serotonin. Serotonin is a powerful chemical (called a neurotransmitter) in your brain that enables you to sleep. L-tryptophan is also the precursor of melatonin, a hormone that also helps the body to sleep.

You can get L-tryptophan in meats (especially turkey), cashews, butter, rice, and whole-grain crackers.

CAFFEINE

Approximately 80 percent of Americans drink at least one cup of coffee or tea a day.[1] Caffeine increases alertness and stimulates the central nervous system. I am not against drinking one or even two cups of organic coffee in the morning, because of the numerous health benefits of coffee. Unfortunately, many Americans are drinking coffee or some other caffeinated beverage in the late afternoon or evening, and that is affecting their sleep. For more information on the caffeine content of some of the popular drinks, please see Day 9 of Pillar 1 in my book *The Seven Pillars of Health*.

It takes about six hours to metabolize half the caffeine in a small cup of coffee.[2] So, if you drink your coffee in the late afternoon or evening, the caffeine will probably stimulate your nervous system and keep you alert during the night, thus prohibiting you from entering the deeper stages of sleep. The more deep sleep you attain usually enables you to awaken more refreshed. If you are suffering from insomnia, limit your coffee intake to one to two cups a day in 8-ounce cups, not 16-ounce size, or approximately 150–300 mg of caffeine a day.

If you have any liver impairment caused by medications such as statin drugs or history of a fatty liver, cut that amount of caffeine in half. If you still have problems with insomnia, keep cutting back your caffeine intake until you have either weaned off coffee or you are sleeping well.

Over-the-counter medications can be packed with caffeine as well. For example, one Excedrin contains 65 mg of caffeine. Cold medications also commonly contain caffeine. So, watch your intake of those products before bedtime.

Chocolate can also keep you up at night. Chocolate ice cream, chocolate cake, chocolate candy bars, chocolate milk, and the like contain caffeine and theobromine, which are both stimulants. Chocolate also contains tyramine and phenylethylamine, which both increase alertness and can contribute to insomnia.

SLEEP SOUNDLY WITH LESS SUGAR AND FEWER CARBS

Caffeine is not the only dietary enemy of sleep. Sugar can be just as bad for your ability to rest. A poor diet of too many simple sugars and processed carbohydrates can also lead to insomnia. We in America eat far too much sugar, and when we eat sugar before going to bed, sleeplessness can be the result.

Americans are now consuming more fat-free foods, which usually means that they are over-consuming highly processed carbohydrates and sugars. Foods high in processed carbohydrates and sugars stimulate insulin release from the pancreas. Insulin in turn triggers the body to store more fat. Insulin may also cause low blood sugar. Low blood sugar then triggers the adrenals to produce more adrenaline and cortisol, which may cause you to be awakened in the middle of the night.

Eating sugar and processed carbohydrates before bedtime often leads to low blood sugar in the middle of the night. This can also happen if you go to bed hungry. You can prevent this dip in blood sugar that wakes you out of sleep by eating a light, well-balanced, high-fiber snack at bedtime. Eating a light evening snack that is correctly balanced with proteins, carbohydrates, fiber, and fats will stabilize blood sugar levels and improve sleep.

> There remaineth therefore a rest to the people of God.
> —HEBREWS 4:9, KJV

You may use whey protein, rice protein, or a vegetarian protein other than soy (such as Life's Basics). These are protein powders that may be mixed with water, coconut milk, skim milk, or plain low-fat kefir. Or you may get plain protein powder such as whey, vegetarian (such as Life's Basics), or rice and make a smoothie with frozen fruit and ice mixed with water, coconut milk, skim milk, or plain low-fat kefir..

A **BIBLE CURE** Recipe

Dr. Colbert's Protein Smoothie

Here's a delicious protein smoothie that you can enjoy at bedtime. Not only will it help you to balance your blood sugar, but it will also improve your health as well.

- 1 scoop protein powder (Life's Basics protein, whey, or rice protein, equal to 14–15 g protein)
- 1–2 Tbsp. of ground flaxseeds
- ¼–½ cup frozen strawberries, raspberries, blackberries, or blueberries, or a combination of them OR
- ½ frozen banana
- 1 cup water, coconut milk or kefir, or organic skim milk or kefir

Blend into a smoothie and enjoy!

LATE-NIGHT EATING AND DRINKING

Eating a large meal close to bedtime can also cause insomnia. Our digestive tract is not designed to digest in a prone or supine (lying) position and works best when we are up and moving around. Our stomach and pancreas are also not designed to be undergoing major digestion of food while we are sleeping. This is another reason we see so much heartburn, indigestion, and acid reflux in America, which also contributes to our insomnia.

Foods containing both tyrosine and tyramine cause insomnia because they are converted in the body to norepinephrine, which is an excitatory neurotransmitter that stimulates us and may keep us awake. Foods high in tyrosine include milk, cheese, yogurt, cottage cheese, soy, peanuts, bananas, turkey, and lima beans. Foods that are high in tyramine include red wine; yogurt; sour cream; aged cheeses; pickled meats; many fish; fermented foods such as soy sauce, sauerkraut, and pickles; figs; raisins; dates; fresh baked breads; and processed meats such as bologna and salami.

Also, consuming too many fatty foods close to bedtime will delay digestion and can cause insomnia. Fats take much longer to digest compared with carbohydrates or proteins.

Many individuals drink one or two glasses of wine at night since it helps them unwind and fall asleep. Yes, alcohol docs help you fall asleep; however, you are more likely to awaken later in the night. Alcohol intake reduces the time spent in stages three and four and REM sleep, which are the most restorative stages of sleep. Alcohol can also worsen snoring. So, alcohol is actually a double-edged sword when it comes to sleep. Also, a major problem with many of my patients is overconsumption of fluids in the evening. As a result they are up two to three times a night urinating. After 7:00 p.m. simply cut back on your fluid intake.

MAINTAINING YOUR IDEAL WEIGHT

Maintaining your ideal weight is critically important for sound sleep. Approximately 66 percent of American adults are either overweight or obese according to federal guidelines.[3] Overweight is defined as a body mass index (BMI) of twenty-five to twenty-nine. Obesity is defined as a body mass index of thirty or more. The body mass index is simply a formula that considers your weight and height to determine if you are healthy, overweight, or obese. For more information on maintaining your ideal weight, refer to *Dr. Colbert's "I Can Do This" Diet* and *The Bible Cure for Weight Loss and Muscle Gain*.

CONCLUSION

One of the most powerful scriptures in the Bible is very short and simple. It says, "This I know, that God is for me" (Ps. 56:9, NAS). If ever you're tossing and turning at night or fighting the symptoms of a particular sleep disorder, let me encourage you to pull up this verse and never forget it. God is for you. He is on your side. He wants you to succeed in every way possible—in body, mind, and spirit.

> At this, I woke up and looked around. My sleep had been very sweet.
> —JEREMIAH 31:26

Before long you'll be declaring with the psalmist, "Return to your rest, O my soul, for the LORD has dealt bountifully with you" (Ps. 116:7, NAS).

A **BIBLE CURE** Prayer for You

Dear Lord, thank You that You are with me in everything that I do. Thank You for Your care and concern in my life. Help me to make all the changes I need to make to my diet. And most of all, if ever I feel all alone in the middle of the night, allow me to feel Your presence to remind me that You're always there. Amen.

A **BIBLE CURE** Prescription

Make a personal plan, based on what you have just read in this chapter, about what food or drink you will remove from your diet and what food or drink you will add to your diet to improve your quality of sleep.

Food/Drink to Remove From Diet	Food/Drink to Add to Diet
1.	1.
2.	2.
3.	3.
4.	4.
5.	5.
6.	6.
7.	7.
8.	8.
9.	9.
10.	10.

REST ASSURED THROUGH GOOD HEALTH HABITS

WE HAVE SEEN how good sleep promotes good health, but realize that good health habits also promote good sleep. Maintaining a healthy diet as we discussed in the last chapter, regular exercise, avoiding cigarettes and excessive intake of alcohol, as well as reducing stress are just a few health habits that enable us to enjoy a good night's sleep. One study found regular exercise is as good for inducing sleep as the use of benzodiazepines, which are prescription sleep medications. Other studies have found that relaxation yoga has special benefits for sleep, including meditation, deep-breathing techniques, and stretching to relax the body and mind.[1] I discuss these topics in detail in my book *The Seven Pillars of Health.*

Dealing with stress and pressure through exercise and a number of valuable lifestyle changes may be all that you need to once again enjoy the refreshing rest you need.

ARE YOU LOSING SLEEP OVER STRESS?

One of the most common causes of insomnia is an excessive amount of stress. We live in such a fast-paced society. We have less and less time to complete more and more tasks. Similar to the ancient Israelites under the harsh rule of Pharaoh, our stressed-out American lifestyle seems to be constantly demanding that we produce more and more bricks with less and less straw.

Many people respond to excess stress by worrying and losing sleep. But not all stress is bad. As a matter of fact, some stress is very good, and the right amount of stress is healthy. To gain more tools to reduce stress in your life, refer to my book *Stress Less*.

AEROBIC EXERCISE

Aerobic exercise such as brisk walking is one of the best ways to improve the quality of your sleep. Aerobic exercise helps you to fall asleep faster and to sleep longer. Those who exercise regularly also spend a greater amount of time in stage three and stage four sleep, which are the most restorative, repairing stages of sleep.

> Therefore I urge you, brethren, by the mercies of God, to present your bodies a living and holy sacrifice, acceptable to God, which is your spiritual service of worship.
>
> —ROMANS 12:1, NAS

By spending more time in stages three and four sleep, you will awaken more refreshed and have much more energy throughout the day. However, don't exercise within three to four hours of bedtime, for this can actually cause insomnia.

Choose an aerobic exercise that you enjoy, and you won't become bored with it. Get a partner—a friend or your spouse— and if you choose walking, vary your experiences by going to different parks or malls for a change of scenery. Walk slowly enough so that you can carry on a conversation but fast enough so that you cannot sing. Over time, you should notice that your sleep improves dramatically.

SLEEP HYGIENE

As you continue to develop good health habits to improve the quality of your sleep, consider adopting good sleep hygiene. Sleep hygiene simply refers to the practices that promote continuous and effective sleep. Another way to look at it is this: sleep hygiene is simply establishing healthy sleep habits. There are twenty-five good sleep hygiene habits that will enable most people to fall asleep and stay asleep.[7]

1. The most important sleep hygiene tip is to establish a regular bedtime as well as a regular time of waking up in the morning. Make this a habit, and stick to the schedule on weekends and even during vacations. Do not be haphazard about it, but based on your work schedule, set aside eight hours for sleep and a time to be in bed. For myself, I choose to be in bed between 10:00 and 10:30 p.m.

2. Use your bed only for sleep and sexual relations. Do not use your bed for reading, watching TV, snacking, working, or worrying.

3. Avoid naps after 3:00 p.m. When they are taken earlier in the day, make sure they are not longer than twenty to thirty minutes.

4. Exercise before dinner. Exercising too close to bedtime disrupts sleep.

5. Avoid caffeine in the late afternoon and evening.

6. Avoid excessive fluids in the late evening and especially before bedtime.

7. Eat normal portion sizes of a well-balanced meal at dinnertime approximately three to four hours before bedtime as well as a light bedtime snack. Do not go to bed hungry, and do not eat a large meal prior to bedtime.

8. Take a warm bath one to two hours before bedtime, and consider adding lavender oil if desired in order to help you relax.

9. Keep the bedroom cool and well ventilated.

10. Purchase a comfortable mattress, pillow, and linens. (Check out a 3-inch Tempur-Pedic pad from Sam's Club to put on top of your mattress.) Remember, you spend roughly one-third of your life in bed; therefore, your bed should be your most important piece of furniture.

11. Thirty minutes before going to bed start to wind down by listening to soothing music, reading the Bible or another good book, having a massage, or being intimate with your spouse.

12. Put dimmer switches on your lights, and dim them a few hours prior to bedtime.

13. After you lie down to go to sleep, if you are not asleep in twenty minutes, simply get up, go into

another room, and read and relax in dim light until you feel sleepy. Then return to bed.

14. If your spouse awakens you with snoring or unusual movements, simply move to the guest bedroom.

15. Try to wake up at the same time each day.

16. Try exchanging foot, neck and shoulder, back, or scalp massages with your spouse, and purchase an inexpensive handheld massager from Brookstone.

17. Relax your mind and body before bedtime by gentle stretching, relaxation exercises, or using an aromatherapy candle or oil.

18. Clean clutter out of the bedroom, and remove computers, fax machines, paperwork, and anything that reminds you of work.

19. Make sure your bedroom is completely dark. Remove all nightlights, and cover your alarm clock and phone light with a hand towel. Put black electrical tape or sticky notepads over tiny lights on your alarm system, TV, DVD, satellite, stereo, or any other lights that are visible. Consider purchasing blackout curtains.

20. Block out noise by using earplugs, double-paning your windows, or using heavy drapes. I personally use a sound generator I purchased from Brookstone that plays white noise. Or you can simply use a fan.

21. Try a lullaby CD or a CD that has sounds of nature.

22. Keep pets out of your bedroom. Pets may snore, pounce on you, growl, howl, bark, or whine. They can also trigger allergies in many patients.

23. Avoid watching heart-pounding movies, ball games, or late-night news. Instead watch something funny or lighthearted before bedtime, but it's best not to watch TV in the bedroom.

24. When lying in bed, you and your spouse may try telling or reading funny jokes to one another. Couples who laugh together and pray together generally stay together.

25. Meditate on Scripture, and do not let your mind worry or wander. I meditate on the Lord's Prayer in Matthew 6:9–13. I also meditate on Psalm 91, 1 Corinthians 13:4–8, and Ephesians 6:10–18. You need to memorize these scriptures and meditate on them over and over.

CONCLUSION

By now you've discovered that many of your daily choices can impact your ability to walk in the wonderful blessing of refreshing, rejuvenating sleep. Enjoying rest is a powerful gift from God. Therefore, always look to Him for blessed rest, for He promises to give you sleep. The Bible says, "It is vain for you to rise up early, to sit up late, to eat the bread of sorrows; for so He gives His beloved sleep" (Ps. 127:2, NKJV).

A **BIBLE CURE** Prayer for You

I thank You, God, that You promised me blessed, quiet, refreshing, and rejuvenating rest because You love me. Show me what lifestyle changes I need to make to walk in the blessings of Your gift of rest. Help me to develop a regular exercise routine, and help me to stick to it once I've begun. I thank You with all my heart for Your great and mighty love for me. Help me to order my life in a way that always pleases You. Amen.

A BIBLE CURE Prescription

Here are ten tremendous tips you can take to help you sleep.[3] Check the ones you plan to use.

❏ Stay away from the big four: caffeine, stress, alcohol, and smoking.

❏ Leave time in your schedule for sleep.

❏ Set a regular sleep schedule, seven days a week. Try to get up at the same time every day.

❏ Relax before going to bed. Reflect on the day, then release your stress and give all your burdens to Jesus (Matt. 11:28–30).

❏ Use your bedroom for sleep only—no work, study, or eating. If the TV causes insomnia, get it out of the bedroom.

❏ Prepare a comfortable sleep environment with a comfortable pillow, mattress, and room temperature. Remove all noise and light from the bedroom.

❏ Start a regular exercise program, but don't exercise for three to four hours before bedtime.

❏ Observe good eating habits. Don't go to bed hungry, and don't drink excessive fluids before bed.

❏ Get up if you can't sleep after twenty to thirty minutes, and go to another room to relax or read. Return to bed when you are tired.

❏ Determine to make sleep a priority and a regular part of your life.

5

REST ASSURED THROUGH PROACTIVE SLEEP THERAPIES

E VERY PERSON AND animal in God's creation must rest. The land and its plants rest as they cycle through seasons. As a foundational principle of Creation, God designed rest to strengthen every aspect of your life and health. The Bible says, "For thus says the Lord GOD, the Holy One of Israel: 'In returning and rest you shall be saved; in quietness and confidence shall be your strength'" (Isa. 30:15, NKJV).

Getting the rest you need is vital to everything you do. Rest heals and restores your body, and rest in God saves or delivers you from the pressures and stress that daily assault your body and mind.

Let's take a look now at some sleep therapies that can get you to sleep restfully without medication or those unpredictable side effects.

LIGHT UP YOUR LIFE!

The body's clock is actually located in a part of the brain called the hypothalamus. Sunlight plays a very important part in influencing your body's clock rhythms, called circadian rhythms, as we discussed in chapter 2. Alarm clocks and artificial light sources such as full spectrum lights can be used to set your body clock and influence your circadian rhythms.

Circadian rhythms are also influenced by the time we choose to go to bed, the time we choose to wake up, the timing of our meals, and the timing of our exercise and of our nightlife.

Circadian rhythms are influenced by many factors that vary from person to person. That's why some of us are early birds and others are night owls, as we discovered in chapter 2. Light therapy is one of the many ways to adjust your internal clock to fit your work schedule and to ensure you are getting the rest you need to stay productive and healthy.

LIGHT THERAPY FOR IMPROVING SLEEP

Believe it or not, how much bright sunlight you get during the day can have a significant impact on how well you sleep!

Most Americans spend way too much time indoors with dim artificial light or florescent lighting. Consequently, we get far too little bright sunlight. This disrupts our circadian clocks, which alters our mood, interferes with our sleep, and affects us both mentally and physically.

Low amounts of natural light exposure for a prolonged period of time may eventually cause an imbalance of the hormones serotonin and melatonin. This can lead to seasonal affective disorder, otherwise known as SAD. SAD involves experiencing a mild depression with symptoms of sadness, hopelessness, lethargy, weight loss or weight gain, and other symptoms of mild depression. This disorder usually occurs during late autumn and winter months when days grow shorter, thus limiting sunlight.

Also called winter depression, SAD affects about 11 million

Americans each year.[1] These people need more sleep; they experience a decreased quality of sleep and wake up tired. Seasonal affective disorder is much more common in the northern part of the United States.

> Casting all your care upon Him, for He cares for you.
> —1 PETER 5:7, NKJV

Getting enough sunlight during the day will help increase melatonin at night. It also helps to increase the neurotransmitters serotonin and norepinephrine. Melatonin and serotonin help to promote sleep, whereas norepinephrine and serotonin also help to elevate your mood.

Spend at least twenty to thirty minutes a day in the sunlight under a shade tree. You can eat lunch outside at a picnic table or inside near a window that allows plenty of sunlight in. If you live in the north where many days are overcast, it might help to purchase a light box that has full-spectrum lights. A much less expensive option is to simply purchase a light visor, which is simply a visor cap with LED lights on it. If you live in sunny southern climates where adequate sunlight is abundant, then sit outside at lunch for approximately thirty minutes under a shade tree and receive the healing power of light as you enjoy your lunch.[2]

Night-shift workers

If you work evenings, night shifts, or rotating shifts, a few changes may help—especially if you work rotating shifts. If you work at night and sleep during the day, be sure to sleep in a completely dark room with all light sealed out. Before you leave for work in the evening, spend time in a light box or wearing a light visor. Finally, when you return home in the morning, wear dark sunglasses that block out all light to prepare the mind and body for sleep.

For those who tend to work crazy hours, napping can be a godsend.

THE POWER OF NAPPING

Research shows that people can increase alertness, reduce stress, and improve concentration and memory with a nap. A power nap also usually improves learning, improves reaction time, and makes you more patient, more efficient, and healthier.

Studies have shown that twenty minutes of sleep in the afternoon is significantly better than twenty minutes of more sleep in the morning. Sleep experts recommend that the nap be approximately twenty minutes in length. A nap longer than this will usually put you into a deeper stage of sleep, making you groggy and more difficult to awaken. Longer naps also actually interfere with sleep.

One study found that the short nap boosted performance by 34 percent and alertness by 54 percent.[3] A twenty-minute power nap in the early to mid afternoon is a great way to boost energy, concentration, and memory, but do not get in the habit of using naps to make up for sleep debt, and do not take a nap if it prevents you from going to bed at your regular time.

Since so many Americans are sleep deprived, napping is one of the best ways for restoring and catching up on sleep.

OTHER SLEEP THERAPIES

To prevent insomnia, you usually need to learn methods to help you relax and fall asleep. There are numerous behavioral methods that do this. These behavioral techniques can relieve chronic insomnia in many cases. Many patients with primary insomnia are helped with behavioral therapy. Medications are equally as effective as behavioral therapy in helping people with insomnia. However, most sleep medications are addictive, have side effects, and are unable to cure insomnia. Behavioral methods work fast and work in all age groups, including children as well as the elderly.

Behavioral techniques include progressive muscle relaxation, biofeedback, cognitive-behavioral therapy, imagery task, sleep restriction, stimulus control, and paradoxical intention. Behavioral method goals are simply to decrease the time it takes to fall to sleep to less than thirty minutes and also to decrease wake-up periods during the night. Of the patients treated with these nondrug methods, 70–80 percent have improved sleep, according to the studies. Even more amazing is that studies report that 75 percent of those taking medications to sleep are able to stop or reduce their use after having behavioral therapy.[4] I go into detail regarding many of these methods in my book *Stress Less*, but let's look at a few of the behavioral methods here.

Cognitive-behavioral therapy (CBT)

Cognitive-behavioral therapy is a form of therapy that teaches patients how to recognize and change negative thought patterns and change the way they interpret events. It has been used in treating anxiety and depression for decades, but it is also very useful in treating insomnia. The patients with insomnia are commonly caught in negative thought patterns regarding sleep. Typical thoughts include:

- "I won't be able to fall asleep."
- "It will take me one or two hours to fall asleep."
- "I must get eight hours of sleep in order to function."
- "If I don't get enough sleep, my job performance will suffer greatly."

As a result of their negative thinking, they usually lie in bed unable to sleep. The treatment goal is to change their distortional thought patterns about their ability to fall asleep and stay asleep. In Mark 11:24, Jesus said, "Therefore I say to you, whatever things you ask when you pray, believe that you receive them, and you will have them" (NKJV). If you believe that you won't be able to fall asleep or sleep through the night, then you won't be able to. However, we have a promise in Psalm 127:2 that says that God gives His beloved sleep. We are actually promised sleep in God's Word. Now, who are you going to side with—God's Word or your fears? According to 2 Corinthians 10:4–5, it is critically important to tear down these mental strongholds, which are our fears and worries about sleep. Then begin to believe, confess, and visualize God giving His beloved (you) sweet sleep. For more information on cognitive-behavioral therapy, please refer to *The New Bible Cure for Depression and Anxiety* and the National Association of Cognitive-Behavioral Therapists at www.nacbt.org.

Progressive muscle relaxation

It takes about ten minutes to perform progressive muscle relaxation, which typically focuses on one muscle group at a time on one side of the body, usually starting in the feet. The muscles are tensed for five to ten seconds, and then the muscle is relaxed for about fifteen seconds. Then simply move up to the next muscle group and repeat the sequence for doing one side of the body at a time. This is discussed in detail in my book *Stress Less*.

Abdominal breathing

Abdominal breathing is also known as diaphragmatic breathing. If you have ever gone to a newborn nursery, you will notice that all newborns are abdominal breathers. However, as we grow older and become more and more stressed, we eventually shift from being abdominal breathers to chest breathers. Chest breathing is stress breathing. However, opera singers and certain other professional singers, as well as musicians who play wind instruments, are usually abdominal breathers. Learn more about abdominal breathing from my book *Stress Less*.

Visual imagery and/or meditation

Visual imagery is simply using your imagination to visualize experiencing something wonderful or a place you would love to visit, such as the beach, a snow-covered mountain resort, a relaxing stream, or a brook. It is very important to use all five senses in order to place yourself in your own special oasis and see it in living color in the theater of your mind. Smell the flowers, hear the sounds of birds and other creatures, feel the sand between your toes, taste the refreshing beverage, and so forth. You can also purchase visual imagery CDs that enable you to retreat to a beautiful getaway in your own mind.

Meditation is also beneficial as a behavioral technique for insomnia. I recommend meditating on the Bible and using scriptures or words such as the fruit of the Spirit. This will be discussed later in this book. For more information on meditation, please see my book *Stress Less*.

Biofeedback

Biofeedback teaches how to control physiologic functions such as muscle tension, heart rate, breathing, blood pressure, skin temperature, perspiration, and even brain waves. By learning to control these functions, you can usually learn to improve your sleep.

There are actually four different types of biofeedback: neurofeedback, EMG biofeedback, respiratory biofeedback, and thermal biofeedback. I find that neurofeedback and EMG biofeedback especially are beneficial to my patients with insomnia.

Other behavioral methods include stimulus control, which helps patients regain the idea that the bed is for sleeping or sexual intercourse, and if unable to fall asleep within twenty minutes, they are instructed to simply get up and go into another room. Sleep restriction is another behavioral method that restricts the time spent in bed but not asleep.

These behavioral methods are very important in treating insomnia. It is very simple to learn progressive muscle relaxation and abdominal breathing as well as visual imagery. I also commonly refer patients to a cognitive-behavioral therapist as well as a biofeedback provider if they continue having problems with insomnia.

CONCLUSION

Taking advantage of sleep therapies to retrain your body's internal clock or to change negative thoughts toward sleep will benefit you in more ways than one. You will find that these strategies will spill over into other parts of your life, creating a stress-free, peaceful, and balanced existence. Follow up on the details for many of these strategies in my book *Stress Less* and *The New Bible Cure for Depression and Anxiety* to really see the far-reaching, lifelong benefits you can attain.

A BIBLE CURE *Prayer for You*

Father God, I thank You for Your infinite wisdom that will help me navigate the best therapy to reshape my thoughts and my sleep habits so that I can have complete and rejuvenating rest in You—mind, body, and spirit. I thank You for revealing these strategies to me. Now I pray that You will give me the strength I need to apply the right ones to my life. Give me the motivation I need to make rest a priority. In Jesus's name I pray, amen.

A **BIBLE CURE** Prescription

Philippians 4:6–7 says, "Be anxious for nothing, but in everything by prayer and supplication, with thanksgiving, let your request be made known to God; and the peace of God, which surpasses all understanding, will guard your hearts and minds through Christ Jesus" (NKJV). The most powerful way to enter into peace and relaxation is practicing thanksgiving. Simply make a gratitude list, and review all of the people and things you are thankful for. Lie in bed and review your list. Also, meditate on God's Word and memorize scriptures. I recommend memorizing the Lord's Prayer in Matthew 6:9–13, Psalm 23, Psalm 91, 1 Corinthians 13:4–8, and Ephesians 6:10–18.

_____

_____

_____

_____

_____

_____

_____

_____

REST ASSURED THROUGH SUPPLEMENTS

G OD PROMISES SWEET sleep to those who conduct their lives with His wisdom. The Bible says, "Keep sound wisdom and discretion, so they will be life to your soul, and adornment to your neck…When you lie down, you will not be afraid; when you lie down, your sleep will be sweet" (Prov. 3:21–22, 24, NAS).

One way to walk in wisdom is to understand good stewardship of your own health by providing your body with all it needs for proper sleep. In addition, learn what nutrients, herbs, and other supplements can help.

Supplementing your diet with vitamins, minerals, herbs, amino acids, and other supplements can dramatically impact many sleep disorders. So let's take a look at a program of supplementation that will make you wiser about helping your body to sleep.

SUPPLEMENTS FOR SOUND SLEEP

To begin a supplementation program, be sure that your body has all the vitamins and minerals it needs to function at optimal levels. Start with a good comprehensive multivitamin/ multimineral supplement.

A good multivitamin/multimineral supplement

I strongly recommend a comprehensive multivitamin and multimineral supplement that contains adequate levels of B vitamins, magnesium, and trace minerals. This will provide optimal nutritional supplementation for a good night's sleep. Divine Health Multivitamin for men and women is an excellent multivitamin.

Several special herbs and other supplements are especially effective in helping you sleep. However, you will find that supplementing with magnesium, melatonin, certain amino acids, herbs, or hormones at bedtime, or drinking teas, is very effective; also, these teas and supplements are nonaddictive, unlike most medications for sleep. Herbs and supplements for sleep are usually used on a short-term basis unless you have anxiety, depression, or a deficiency in melatonin or certain calming neurotransmitters. Let's look at some of these helpful supplements.

Melatonin

Melatonin is a hormone produced by a small gland, called the pineal gland, in the brain. Melatonin helps to regulate sleep and wake cycles, or circadian rhythms. Usually melatonin begins to rise in the evening and remains high for most of the night and then decreases in the early morning. Melatonin production is affected by light. As a person ages, melatonin levels decline. Older adults typically produce very small amounts of melatonin or none at all. Studies suggest that melatonin induces sleep without suppressing REM or dream sleep, whereas most sleep meds suppress REM sleep.[1]

Melatonin works best if the patient's melatonin levels are low. Children generally have normal levels of melatonin; therefore, supplementation with melatonin in children usually is ineffective. However, in adults, especially the elderly, it may be very effective in treating insomnia and is excellent in treating jet lag. It is also usually very effective for those who work the night shift.

A **BIBLE CURE** *Health Fact*

Melatonin is also a powerful antitoxin that fights certain types of cancer and helps protect cells during chemotherapy. See *The Bible Cure for Cancer* for more information.

The main side effect of melatonin is sleepiness, which is good; however, other potential side effects include vivid dreams, morning grogginess, and headaches. The recommended dose of melatonin is typically 1–6 mg at bedtime. I recommend a melatonin lozenge since it dissolves in the mouth and seems to work better for most patients. I start my patients on a low dose and gradually increase the dose until the patient is sleeping well. I also commonly continue melatonin with other natural sleep aids that you will be soon learning about. Remember, melatonin as well as other sleep aids work best when practicing good sleep hygiene.

L-tryptophan and 5-HTP (5-hydroxytryptophan)

I commonly place patients with insomnia on melatonin and the amino acid L-tryptophan or 5-HTP. L-tryptophan improves sleep normalcy and increases stage four sleep (the most restorative stage of sleep). It has also been shown to improve obstructive sleep apnea in many patients, and it does not decrease cognitive performance.

Both L-tryptophan and its metabolite 5-HTP are used to increase serotonin levels in the brain. Serotonin is a neurotransmitter in the brain that promotes restful sleep and well-being as well as satiety.

However, when serotonin levels are low in the brain, you are more prone to experience insomnia. Serotonin levels are also increased by ingesting carbohydrates. When carbohydrates are ingested with L-tryptophan or 5-HTP, the elevated insulin level increases the removal of other amino acids that compete with tryptophan and 5-HTP for transport into the brain. Carbohydrates also tend to increase the sedative effects of 5-HTP and tryptophan.

I recommend vitamin B_6, niacin, and magnesium, which serve as cofactors in the conversion of L-tryptophan and 5-HTP to serotonin. I usually recommend simply taking either 1,000–2,000 mg of L-tryptophan or 100–300 mg of 5-HTP at bedtime. In addition, I recommend a comprehensive multivitamin that contains adequate amounts of vitamin B_6, niacin, and magnesium, which helps convert L-tryptophan and 5-HTP to serotonin. Also, I usually have the patients take their L-tryptophan or 5-HTP with a food that is high in carbohydrate and low in protein, such as a Fiber One bar.

L-theanine and GABA

I have found that most patients with insomnia are under excessive stress and may be suffering from anxiety and depression. Excessive stress, anxiety, and depression are usually associated with elevated cortisol levels, especially at night. Elevated stress hormones, especially cortisol, eventually disrupt brain chemistry, causing imbalances in neurotransmitters, including serotonin, dopamine, norepinephrine, and GABA, as well as other brain chemicals.

However, the amino acid L-theanine crosses the blood-brain barrier and is able to suppress stress hormones, including cortisol. L-theanine is one of the natural chemicals found in green tea and helps to decrease stress and anxiety. It also helps the body produce other calming neurotransmitters, including GABA, serotonin, and dopamine. In Japan, L-theanine is usually added to sodas and chewing gum to provide a relaxing and soothing effect.[2]

I find that L-theanine typically works better with the amino acid GABA. GABA is also a calming neurotransmitter in the brain that has a soothing effect on the nervous system. L-theanine and GABA supplements taken with vitamin B_6 usually help to calm the mind as well as lower the stress hormones and help you fall asleep. I usually recommend 200–400 mg of L-theanine with 500–1,000 mg of GABA at bedtime taken with a comprehensive multivitamin containing vitamin B_6. This combination may also be taken with melatonin and 5-HTP or L-tryptophan. For more information on GABA, please see *The New Bible Cure for Depression and Anxiety.*

Magnesium

We already know that adequate amounts of magnesium are needed to help convert L-tryptophan and 5-HTP to serotonin. There is also a close association between normal sleep architecture and magnesium. The excitatory neurotransmitter glutamate disrupts normal sleep architecture, causing insomnia, whereas the inhibitory neurotransmitter GABA usually improves sleep architecture. Magnesium is a mineral that helps decrease the glutamate activity in the brain while at the same time increasing the GABA activity in the brain. This usually helps to improve sleep. Thus, magnesium is able to help many patients with insomnia issues.

I commonly recommend a magnesium powder, Natural Calm, to patients with insomnia. Simply taking 1½ teaspoons of Natural Calm in 4 ounces of hot water as a tea at bedtime provides 307 mg of magnesium and helps many of my patients fall asleep.

Other teas to treat insomnia

For centuries, people have used chamomile tea to treat insomnia. Chamomile tea is a mild muscle relaxant and has mild sedative properties; it may also help relieve stress, anxiety, and depression. It usually helps promote a deep sleep as well as feelings of relaxation and calmness. The active ingredients are volatile oils found in the flowers of chamomile.

Sleepytime Tea blends floral Egyptian chamomile with cool spearmint from the Pacific Northwest and Guatemalan lemongrass. Another tea called Tilo, also known as linden flower tea, has gentle relaxing properties that help to relieve stress and may help relieve anxiety. In choosing teas, always choose organic teas. Many of my patients use these teas as sleep aids and have found them to be very beneficial in treating insomnia. However, a word of caution: people who are allergic to ragweed should avoid chamomile and Sleepytime Tea.

Valerian root

Valerian root is another herb that has been used for many years for insomnia; it also helps to calm the mind. It is believed that valerian works by increasing GABA levels in the brain. With its mild sedative qualities, valerian helps people fall asleep and improve their quality of sleep. It may take two to three weeks to appreciate its full effect. Valerian root may be taken as pills or tea; however, the tea has a very unpleasant taste. If you choose any herbal supplement including valerian, make sure it is organic.

Unlike medications, no standard dosing guidelines have been established for valerian root. For treating insomnia, a valerian root dosage that is sometimes recommended is 300–900 mg per day. It's best to take it thirty minutes to two hours before bedtime.

Magnolia bark and adaptogens

Magnolia bark, *magnolia officinalis,* a traditional Chinese medicine, has been used for thousands of years to help with low energy, emotional distress, digestive problems, diarrhea, and more. Modern research has focused on magnolia for its sedative and muscle relaxant properties. Magnolia especially helps patients who are under a lot of stress or who suffer from anxiety.

Adaptogens are substances that help the body adapt to stress by balancing the adrenal glands' response to stress. Adaptogens include rhodiola, ashwagandha, ginseng, and many more. Since excessive stress is a major cause of insomnia, adaptogens given in the evening may be effective in calming the mind and body. For more information on adaptogens, refer to my book *Stress Less.*

Progesterone

Numerous studies have shown that over 50 percent of all peri-menopausal and postmenopausal women have problems falling asleep or staying asleep.[3] This is commonly due to fluctuating levels or low levels of estrogen and progesterone. We also know that women experiencing hot flashes and night sweats usually have a poorer quality of sleep. Bioidentical hormone therapy is one of the simplest yet most profound ways to improve sleep in perimenopausal and postmenopausal women.

Estrogen has an excitatory effect on the brain, whereas progesterone has a calming and soothing effect on the brain. Women with estrogen dominance, which is common prior to menopause, usually experience restless sleep, whereas proges-terone replacement usually dramatically improves sleep. Studies show that progesterone has antianxiety effects by stimulating GABA receptors in the brain.[4] This in turn helps you relax and sleep. GABA also helps balance excitation with inhibition. Researchers have found that progesterone produces a sleep brain wave pattern similar to that of tranquilizers.[5]

I usually check hormone levels in women with insomnia and commonly find low progesterone levels. I check the serum progesterone on day twenty-one of their menstrual cycle. Then I start them on 100 mg of bioidentical progesterone (not synthetic progesterone) at bedtime. Progesterone also must be balanced with bioidentical estrogen. To find a physician who is knowl-edgeable about bioidentical hormone replacement therapy, refer to www.WorldHealth.net.

I want to emphasize that herbs and supplementation should usually be used on a short-term basis unless you have anxiety or depression or if you are over the age of fifty and are deficient in melatonin.

SUPPLEMENTS FOR OTHER SLEEP DISORDERS

Since so many sleep disorders exist, let's look beyond insomnia to some supplements that help relieve the less-common sleep disorders.

Restless legs syndrome

If you are experiencing restless legs syndrome, get your doctor to test you to see if your body is low in iron. A test called a ferritin level blood test can measure the iron stores in your body. If your ferritin level is low, supplementing with iron may relieve restless legs syndrome. Regular aerobic exercise, leg massages, and warm baths with Epsom salts, 1 to 4 cups in the bathwater, can also help relieve the symptoms of restless legs syndrome. Also supplementation with magnesium at bedtime may help. See suggested dosage of magnesium on the next page.

Periodic limb movement disorder

Periodic limb movement disorder is another movement disorder associated with insomnia. This involuntary disorder often causes repetitive, jerking twitches of the legs that last between one and three seconds. This twitching can wake up the sleeper or his or her spouse. Those with this disorder tend to feel quite drowsy throughout the day.

Here are some supplements that may help:

- 400 mg of magnesium in the form of magnesium citrate, magnesium aspartate, or magnesium glycinate OR
- 1–2 tsp. of Natural Calm in 4 oz. of hot water at bedtime

In addition, taking a warm bath and adding 1–4 cups of Epsom salts to the bathwater may also help.

SHOULD I ASK MY DOCTOR FOR MEDICATIONS FOR SLEEP?

I do not routinely recommend pharmaceutical medications for insomnia since they often have side effects. These include addiction or dependence upon the drug, rebound insomnia, and disrupting the normal architecture of sleep.

Rebound insomnia occurs when the insomnia becomes even worse after you go off the medication. Disrupting sleep architecture means that some sleep medications will make you fall asleep, but you will not spend adequate time in the deeper stages of sleep, such as stages three and four. Instead, most of your sleep time will be spent in the superficial stages, such as stages one and two.

Night owls or patients with delayed sleep phase syndrome who stay up late at night may greatly benefit from one or two weeks of a sleep medication to get them used to going to sleep at an earlier time. It is critical that they continue to go to bed at the same time each night. Rozerem is a sleep medicine that helps to shift the circadian rhythm. Ambien may also help, but it is absolutely critical to maintain good sleep hygiene.

CONCLUSION

The promise of living wisely includes enjoying the benefits of refreshing, restoring sweet sleep. Dragging through your days fatigued and tossing through your nights awake is not healthy or wise. But knowledge and wisdom are really never far away from any one of us. As a matter of fact, the Bible says that wisdom is everywhere—we just need to open our ears and hear it. The Word of God says, "Wisdom shouts in the streets. She cries out in the public square. She calls out to the crowds along the main street, to those gathered in front of the city gate.... 'Come and listen to my counsel. I'll share my heart with you and make you wise'" (Prov. 1:20–21, 23).

Why not simply ask the Lord to give you a wise and understanding heart?

A **BIBLE CURE** Prayer for You

Dear Lord, open my ears and my mind to Your wisdom. You have given me the precious gift of health. Help me to be a wise and disciplined steward of that wonderful gift. Show me what supplements my body may be lacking, and help me to support the natural, God-given sleep that You intended for me to enjoy with the right program of supplements. Amen.

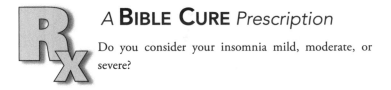

A **BIBLE CURE** Prescription

Do you consider your insomnia mild, moderate, or severe?

_____

_____

_____

_____

I plan to take the following supplements for my sleep disorder:

- ❏ A good multivitamin/multimineral supplement such as Divine Health Multivitamin
- ❏ Melatonin
- ❏ L-tryptophan
- ❏ 5-HTP
- ❏ L-theanine
- ❏ GABA
- ❏ Magnesium
- ❏ Valerian root
- ❏ Progesterone
- ❏ Chamomile or Sleepytime Tea

It is best to start with a multivitamins and L-tryptophan or 5-HTP, then add only one supplement at a time. Do not take all of these natural sleep aids at once, and do not take them with alcohol, sleep medication, or antidepressants. Discuss your supplements with your physician.

REST ASSURED THROUGH REST IN GOD

OW MUCH STRESS you experience in your daily life does not truly indicate how well you will sleep. One person's life can be full of stress-producing events and situations, and yet this person will be at rest. Another individual's life can be comparatively free of stress, and yet this individual might be filled with tension, turmoil, panic, and distress. The difference between the two individuals is not how much stress they encounter, but rather whether or not they are abiding in the vine.

Let me explain. The Bible says, "Remain in me [Jesus], and I will remain in you. For a branch cannot produce fruit if it is severed from the vine, and you cannot be fruitful unless you remain in me. Yes, I am the vine; you are the branches. Those who remain in me, and I in them, will produce much fruit" (John 15:4–5).

Having peace comes from abiding in Christ. This simply means giving Him all of your anxiety, care, and concern and receiving from Him His wisdom, peace, power, and love. This wonderful spiritual exchange produces blessed rest in God.

So you can see that what really matters is not the amount of stress in your life but how you actually perceive that stress and react to it. If you react with worry, anger, rage, fear, resentment, or any other deadly emotion, you're liable to lose a lot of sleep. But if you react to the stress in your life with faith, trust, peace, and reassurance that God is in control, you'll continue to sleep like a baby through every ripple and wave you encounter.

Still, appearances can be deceiving. Sometimes a person who appears calm outwardly can be steaming internally. But it's often difficult to mask your emotions at 2:00 a.m. when you are lying awake staring at the ceiling, replaying the day or planning tomorrow. So if you are struggling to get a good night's sleep, your reactions to stress and other deadly emotions may be a key factor.

Therefore, be sure that you're abiding in the vine. Let's examine some important ways of abiding in the vine.

ABIDING IN THE WORD OF GOD

Psalm 127:2 says, "It is vain for you to rise up early, to sit up late, to eat the bread of sorrows; for so He gives His beloved sleep" (NKJV). The Bible actually promises us a good night's sleep, but we have to do our part in order to obtain it. We unknowingly eat the bread of sorrows by rehashing the stresses and worries of the day and being more concerned about things for tomorrow. We lie in bed at night trying to figure things out. That is vain!

Instead, we need to meditate on God's Word and not on our problems and stresses. As we meditate on God's Word, our problems go. But as we meditate on the problem, our problems grow, and as a result, our sleep is destroyed. Isaiah 26:3 says, "You will keep him in perfect peace, whose mind is stayed on You" (NKJV). In other words, as we keep our minds on God's Word and not our problems, we will enter into peace.

Our minds must be renewed, just as Romans 12:1–2 says, so that they will be on the side of the Spirit, who is perfect. This renewing of the mind occurs as our thoughts are filled with the powerful, living Word of God. But if our minds are always thinking upon negatives, such as what makes us worry or angry, what we don't have that we want, who has hurt us or caused us harm, and what we dislike, then our minds and thoughts are carnal or inspired by our lower nature. When we fill our minds with God's words and thoughts through the Bible and prayer, we feed and strengthen our spirit man, which was designed to serve God.

UNDERSTANDING AND OBEYING THE LAW OF REST

One of the best ways to wind down is to understand and follow God's law of rest. Let's take a look at this incredible law. The Word of God says, "And six years thou shalt sow thy land, and shalt gather the fruits thereof: but the seventh year thou shalt let it rest and lie still.... Six days thou shalt do thy work, and on the seventh day thou shalt rest" (Exod. 23:10–12, KJV).

> For I have given rest to the weary and joy to the sorrowing.
>
> —JEREMIAH 31:25

You can find this same powerful spiritual principle in Exodus 31:15: "Six days may work be done; but in the seventh is the sabbath of rest, holy to the LORD: whosoever doeth any work in the sabbath day, he shall surely be put to death" (KJV). The next verse goes on to say that this was a perpetual covenant—which means that this principle of Sabbath rest never ends. And verse 17 says, "It is a sign between me and the children of Israel *for ever:* for in six days the LORD made heaven and earth, and on the seventh day he rested, and was refreshed" (KJV, emphasis added).

Today we are not under law, but we live under the grace of God that was purchased for us by Christ Jesus. Nevertheless, rest remains a spiritual principle that we cannot disregard without suffering heavy consequences in terms of our health and well-being.

Although we don't honor the Sabbath by strictly forbidding work on Sundays, we enter into a rest when we learn to depend upon God for everything in our lives. The New Testament talks about this rest when it says, "So there remains a Sabbath rest for the people of God" (Heb. 4:9, NAS).

So you can see that rest remains a very present and powerful spiritual principle that God gave to strengthen our bodies and minds and renew our health and spirits. By honoring the Sabbath rest of God, we rest our bodies and our minds. We refuse to carry around the weight of the daily tension, anxiety, fear, and stress of the world. Instead, we let God carry it for us. In doing so, we enter God's rest.

The powerful spiritual principle of God's rest allows our minds and bodies to heal from the effects of stress. Jesus says, "Come to me, all of you who are weary and carry heavy burdens, and I will give you rest" (Matt. 11:28).

God's rest is a vital key factor in living in God's divine health for your body, mind, and soul.

We need to enter into the sleep and rest of Jesus. In Matthew 8, Jesus and His disciples got in a boat, and suddenly a great tempest, or storm, arose on the sea. The wind was probably howling and the boat was rocking violently. The Bible says in verse 24 that the boat was covered with waves, or in other words, it was about to sink. But in spite of the violent rocking of the boat, the howling winds, and the waves crashing over the boat, Jesus was sound asleep. No doubt, He was in stage four sleep, which is the deepest stage of sleep. But then His disciples came and woke Him up and said to Him, "Lord, save us! We are perishing!" He then asked them, "Why are you fearful, O you of little faith?" He then got up and rebuked the winds and the sea, and there was a great calm. The key here is that we too can enter into His rest and sweet sleep just like Jesus if we abide in Him and He abides in us.

A **BIBLE CURE** Prayer for You

Dear Lord, I pray for supernatural rest that refreshes my body, mind, soul, and spirit. I choose to take Your yoke. Teach me to know You and to walk in Your wonderful ways. If ever I find myself struggling to enter Your place of rest, I pray before-hand that You meet me at the point of that struggle and give me inner peace and comfort, just as Jesus had during the storm, and that I'll make it safely to the other side. Amen.

A **BIBLE CURE** Prescription

Personalize the following verse of Scripture by filling your own name in the blanks:

The Lord is _____ shepherd; I have all that I need. He lets _____ rest in green meadows; he leads me beside peaceful streams. He renews _____ strength. He guides me along right paths, bringing honor to his name. Even when I walk through the darkest valley, I will not be afraid, for you are close beside _____. Your rod and your staff protect and comfort me. You prepare a feast for _____ in the presence of my enemies. You honor _____ by anointing my head with oil. My cup overflows with blessings. Surely your goodness and unfailing love will pursue _____ all the days of my life, and _____ will live in the house of the Lord forever.

—Adapted from Psalm 23

A PERSONAL NOTE
From Don Colbert

GOD DESIRES TO heal you of disease. His Word is full of promises that confirm His love for you and His desire to give you His abundant life. His desire includes more than physical health for you; He wants to make you whole in your mind and spirit as well as through a personal relationship with His Son, Jesus Christ.

If you haven't met my best friend, Jesus, I would like to take this opportunity to introduce Him to you. It is very simple. If you are ready to let Him come into your life and become your best friend, all you need to do is sincerely pray this prayer:

> *Lord Jesus, I want to know You as my Savior and Lord. I believe You are the Son of God and that You died for my sins. I also believe You were raised from the dead and now sit at the right hand of the Father praying for me. I ask You to forgive me for my sins and change my heart so that I can be Your child and live with You eternally. Thank You for Your peace. Help me to walk with You so that I can begin to know You as my best friend and my Lord. Amen.*

If you have prayed this prayer, you have just made the most important decision of your life. I rejoice with you in your decision and your new relationship with Jesus. Please contact my publisher at pray4me@charismamedia.com so that we can send you some materials that will help you become established in your relationship with the Lord. We look forward to hearing from you.

CONFESSIONS FOR SLEEP

Scripture	My Confession
"In peace I will lie down and sleep, for you alone, O Lord, will keep me safe" (Ps. 4:8).	The Lord is watching over me and promises me peace, safety, and a good night's sleep. I receive peaceful sleep by faith.
"It is vain for you to rise up early, to sit up late, to eat the bread of sorrows; for so He gives His beloved sleep" (Ps. 127:2, NKJV).	I am God's loved one, and He promises me rest. Thank You, Lord, for rest and sweet sleep as part of my inheritance and a free gift. I receive deep sleep by faith.
"You can go to bed without fear; you will lie down and sleep soundly" (Prov. 3:24).	I will not fear when I lie down because the peace of God rests on me. When I lie down, I will fall asleep, and my sleep will be peaceful, deep, and refreshing just like the sleep of Jesus.
"You will keep him in perfect peace, whose mind is stayed on You, because he trusts in You" (Isa. 26:3, NKJV).	I have perfect peace because my mind is focused on Jesus and not on my problems.

Scripture	My Confession
"Then Jesus said, 'Come to me, all of you who are weary and carry heavy burdens, and I will give you rest'" (Matt. 11:28).	I give all my burdens to Jesus, and I enter into His rest. I have the peace of God and am able to sleep soundly.
"[Jesus said,] 'I am leaving you with a gift—peace of mind and heart. And the peace I give is a gift the world cannot give. So don't be troubled or afraid'" (John 14:27).	I receive the peace of God, the same peace that Jesus had by faith. That was the peace that enabled Him to be in a deep sleep in the midst of a bad storm at sea. His peace rests on me.
"Casting down arguments and every high thing that exalts itself against the knowledge of God, bringing every thought into captivity to the obedience of Christ" (2 Cor. 10:5, NKJV).	I cast every worrisome thought and all other bothersome thoughts out of my mind, and I choose to focus on the name of Jesus. I slowly inhale and exhale as I think the name of Jesus, and I do not allow any other thoughts into my mind.
"Be anxious for nothing, but in everything by prayer and supplication, with thanksgiving, let your requests be made known to God; and the peace of God, which surpasses all understanding, will guard your hearts and minds through Christ Jesus" (Phil. 4:6–7, NKJV).	The peace of God guards my heart and my mind. All thoughts contrary to God's Word are cast out of my mind by faith. Tormenting thoughts must leave, and I refuse to rehash those thoughts. I refuse to be anxious.

Scripture	My Confession
"For God has not given [me] a spirit of fear, but of power and of love and of a sound mind" (2 Tim. 1:7, NKJV).	By faith I have a sound mind. No fear, anxiety, depression, insomnia, or worrisome thoughts can stay because God's Word says I have a sound mind.
"For only we who believe can enter his rest" (Heb. 4:3).	I believe and have entered into God's rest and peace.

RESOURCES FOR SLEEP DISORDERS

Divine Health nutritional products
   1908 Boothe Circle
   Longwood, FL 32750
   Phone: (407) 331-7007
   Web Site: www.drcolbert.com
   E-mail: info@drcolbert.com

Comprehensive multivitamin
   Divine Health Living Multivitamin and Divine Health Multivitamin

Sleep support

- Amino acids: Divine Health 5-HTP, Divine Health Serotonin Max, L-Theanine, GABA, TryptoPure

- Melatonin: Divine Health Melatonin (1 mg and 3 mg)

- Magnesium: Natural Calm, Divine Health Chelated Magnesium

- Adaptogens: Divine Health Stress Manager (magnolia bark), Divine Health Relora Plus

- Sleep herbs: Divine Health Sleep Formula

From health food store
   Chamomile tea and Sleepytime Tea

NOTES

Preface
A Brand-New Bible Cure for a Brand-New You!

1. Jeanne Wright, "A Short Trip From Fatigue to Felony," *Los Angeles Times*, February 16, 2005, http://articles.latimes.com/2005/feb/16/autos/hy-wheels16 (accessed August 10, 2009).

2. American Psychological Association, "Why Sleep Is Important and What Happens When You Don't Get Enough," http://www.apa.org/topics/why.aspx (accessed January 16, 2013).

3. Ibid.

4. Division of Sleep Medicine at Harvard Medical School, "Judgment and Safety," http://healthysleep.med.harvard.edu/need-sleep/whats-in-it-for-you/judgment-safety#2 (accessed August 10, 2009).

Chapter 1
Rest Assured—You Can Find Rest!

1. Lawrence J. Epstein, MD, with Steven Mardon, *The Harvard Medical School Guide to a Good Night's Sleep* (New York: McGraw-Hill, 2007), 5.

2. Ibid., 4.

3. Ibid., 5.

4. Ibid., 4.

5. Insomnia911.com, "Insomnia Statistics," http://www.insomnia911.com/insomnia-facts/statistics.htm (accessed August 11, 2009).

6. National Heart Lung and Blood Institute, "Insomnia: Who Is at Risk for Insomnia?" Insomnia in Women and African Americans, http://www.nhlbi.nih.gov/health/dci/Diseases/inso/inso_whoisatrisk.html (accessed August 11, 2009).

7. Insomnia911.com, "Insomnia Statistics."

8. Ibid.; SleepMed.md, "Sleep Disorders: Sleep Statistics," http://www
   .sleepmed.md/page/1896 (accessed August 11, 2009).

9. Insomnia911.com, "Insomnia Statistics."

10. Ibid.

11. SleepMed.md, "Sleep Disorders: Sleep Statistics."

12. Ibid.

13. Ibid.

14. Gregg D. Jacobs, *Say Good Night to Insomnia* (New York: Henry Holt
    and Company, LLC, 1998), 21.

15. Texas Sleep Medicine, "Insomnia," http://www.txsleepmedicine.com/
    insomnia.html (accessed August 12, 2009).

16. Epstein, *The Harvard Medical School Guide to a Good Night's Sleep*, 5.

17. Ibid., 35.

18. Ibid., 6.

19. Ibid.

20. WebMD.com, "Physical Side Effects of Oversleeping," Sleep
    Disorders Health Center, http://www.webmd.com/sleep-disorders/
    physical-side-effects-oversleeping (accessed August 11, 2009).

21. Ibid.

22. Ibid.

23. WebMD.com, "Older Women's Stroke Risk Linked to Sleep," Stroke
    Health Center, http://www.webmd.com/stroke/news/20080717/older
    -womens-stroke-risk-linked-to-sleep (accessed August 11, 2009).

CHAPTER 2

REST ASSURED BY BEING INFORMED ABOUT SLEEP DISORDERS

1. National Heart Lung and Blood Institute "What Is Insomnia?" U.S.
   Department of Health and Human Service, http://www.nhlbi.nih
   .gov/health/dci/Diseases/inso/inso_whatis.html (accessed August 11,
   2009).

2. SleepMed.md, "Sleep Disorders: Sleep Statistics."

3. H. Klar Yaggi, John Concato, Walter N. Kernan, et al., "Obstructive Sleep Apnea as a Risk Factor for Stroke and Death," *New England Journal of Medicine* 353, no. 19 (November 10, 2005): 2034–2041, abstract accessed at http://content.nejm.org/cgi/content/short/353/19/2034 (accessed August 11, 2009).

4. Associated Press, "Sleep Apnea May Have Contributed to Death," ESPN.com, December 28, 2004, http://sports.espn.go.com/nfl/news/story?id=1953876 (accessed August 10, 2009).

5. Carlos H. Schenck, MD, *Sleep* (New York: Avery, 2008), 36.

6. American Sleep Association, "Sleep Apnea," http://www.sleepassociation.org/index.php?p=sleepapneapublic (accessed August 12, 2009).

7. Medline Plus, "Obstructive Sleep Apnea," http://www.nlm.nih.gov/medlineplus/ency/article/000811.htm (accessed August 12, 2009).

8. Max Hirshkowitz, PhD, DABSM, and Patricia B. Smith, *Sleep Disorders for Dummies* (Hoboken, NJ: Wiley Publishing, Inc., 2004), 184.

9. SleepMed.md, "Sleep Disorders: Sleep Statistics."

10. National Institute of Neurological Disorders and Stroke, "Narcolepsy Fact Sheet," http://www.ninds.nih.gov/disorders/narcolepsy/detail_narcolepsy.htm#58833201 (accessed August 11, 2009).

11. Epstein, *The Harvard Medical School Guide to a Good Night's Sleep*, 157.

12. Ibid.

13. National Institute of Neurological Disorders and Stroke, "Restless Legs Syndrome Fact Sheet," http://www.ninds.nih.gov/disorders/restless_legs/detail_restless_legs.htm (accessed August 11, 2009).

14. Epstein, *The Harvard Medical School Guide to a Good Night's Sleep*, 147.

15. Herbert Ross, DC, with Keri Brenner, LAc, *Alternative Medicine Magazine's Definitive Guide to Sleep Disorders* (Berkeley, CA: Celestial Arts, 2000, 2007), 27.

16. Anna H. Wu, Renwei Wang, Woon-Puay Koh, et al., "Sleep Duration, Melatonin, and Breast Cancer Among Chinese Women in Singapore," *Carcinogenesis* 29, no. 6 (2008): 1244–1248, http://carcin .oxfordjournals.org/cgi/content/full/29/6/1244 (accessed August 12, 2009).

17. Ron Chepesiuk, "Missing the Dark: Health Effects of Light Pollution," *Environmental Health Perspectives* 117, no. 1 (January 2009), http://www.ehponline.org/members/2009/117-1/focus.html (accessed August 12, 2009).

18. Press Release, "IARC Monographs Programme Finds Cancer Hazards Associated With Shiftwork, Painting and Firefighting," The International Agency for Research on Cancer, December 5, 2007, http://www.iarc.fr/en/media-centre/pr/2007/pr180.html (accessed August 12, 2009).

19. Professor Russel Reiter, University of Texas, "Light at Night, Melatonin and Experimental Leukemia Progression," Children With Leukemia, March 2008, http://www.leukaemia.org/what-we-do/ fund-research/prevention-project/completed-prevention-projects/961 (accessed August 12, 2009).

20. Epstein, *The Harvard Medical School Guide to a Good Night's Sleep*, 171.

21. Hirshkowitz and Smith, *Sleep Disorders for Dummies*, 254.

22. Epstein, *The Harvard Medical School Guide to a Good Night's Sleep*, 169.

23. Hirshkowitz and Smith, *Sleep Disorders for Dummies*, 237–238.

24. Epstein, *The Harvard Medical School Guide to a Good Night's Sleep*, 179.

25. Ibid., 172–173.

26. Ibid., 173–174.

CHAPTER 3
REST ASSURED THROUGH PROPER NUTRITION

1. G. W. Ross, R. D. Abbott, H. Petrovitch, L. R. White, and C. M. Tanner, "Relationship Between Caffeine Intake and Parkinson Disease," *Journal of the American Medical Association* 284, no. 11 (September 2000): 1378–1379.

2. Dr. Gregg D. Jacobs, "Lifestyle Practices That Can Improve Sleep (Part 2)," Talk About Sleep, http://www.talkaboutsleep.com/sleep -disorders/archives/insomnia_drjacobs_lifestyle_practices_part2.htm (accessed August 12,2009).

3. Center for Disease Control, "Prevalence of Overweight and Obesity Among Adults: United States, 2003–2004," National Center for Health Statistics, April 2006, http://www.cdc.gov/nchs/products/ pubs/pubd/hestats/overweight/overwght_adult_03.htm (accessed August 12, 2009).

CHAPTER 4
REST ASSURED THROUGH GOOD HEALTH HABITS

1. University of Maryland Medical Center, "Insomnia—Treatment: Sleep Hygiene Tips," http://www.umm.edu/patiented/articles/what_ behavioral_other_non-drug_treatments_insomnia_000027_7.htm (accessed August 12, 2009).

2. Some points in this list have been adapted from University of Maryland Medical Center, "Insomnia—Treatment: Sleep Hygiene Tips."

3. Personalized Sleep Plan Checklist, from *Good Night America: Deep Sleep Reference Guide* (n.p.: Good Night America LLC, 1998).

CHAPTER 5
REST ASSURED THROUGH PROACTIVE SLEEP THERAPIES

1. Hara Estroff Marano, "New Light on Seasonal Depression," *Psychology Today*, November 1, 2003, http://www.psychologytoday.com/articles/200311/new-light-seasonal-depression (accessed August 12, 2009).

2. For more information about full-spectrum lights or light boxes, call the SunBox Company at (800) 548-3968 or Environmental Lighting Concepts, Inc. (OttLite Technology) at (800) 842-8848.

3. S. Lynne Walker, "More Americans Are Waking Up to the Benefits of Midday Snooze," SignOnSanDiego.com, September 4, 2007, http://www.signonsandiego.com/news/nation/20070924-9999-1n24sleep.html (accessed August 12, 2009).

4. University of Maryland Medical Center, "Insomnia—Treatment: Behavioral Therapy Methods," http://www.umm.edu/patiented/articles/what_behavioral_other_non-drug_treatments_insomnia_000027_7.htm (accessed August 12, 2009).

CHAPTER 6
REST ASSURED THROUGH SUPPLEMENTS

1. I. V. Zhdanova, R. J. Wurtman, H. J. Lynch, et al., "Sleep-inducing Effects of Low Doses of Melatonin Ingested in the Evening," *Clinical Pharmacology and Therapeutics* 57, no. 5 (May 1995): 552–558, http://www.ncbi.nlm.nih.gov/pubmed/7768078 (accessed August 13, 2009).

2. Discover Nutrition, "Rapid Anxiety and Stress Relief," http://www.discovernutrition.com/l-theanine.html (accessed August 12, 2009).

3. Aeron Lifecycles Clinical Laboratory, "Sleepless Night, Irritable Days, and Fatigue? It Could Be Your Hormones," *Hormonal Update* 2, no. 12, http://www.aeron.com/volume_2_number_12.htm (accessed August 12, 2009).

4. O. Picazo and A. Fernández-Guasti, "Anti-anxiety Effects of Progesterone and Some of Its Reduced Metabolites: An Evaluation Using the Burying Behavior Test," *Brain Research* 680, nos. 1–2 (1995):135–141, http://www.biomedexperts.com/Abstract.bme/7663969/Anti-anxiety_effects_of_progesterone_and_some_of_its_reduced_metabolites_an_evaluation_using_the_burying_behavior_test (accessed August 13, 2009).

5. A. H. Söderpalm, S. Lindsey, R. H. Purdy, et al, "Administration of Progesterone Produces Mild Sedative-like Effects in Men and Women," *Psychoneuroendocrinology* 29, no. 3 (April 2004): 339–354.

Don Colbert, MD, was born in Tupelo, Mississippi. He attended Oral Roberts School of Medicine in Tulsa, Oklahoma, where he received a bachelor of science degree in biology in addition to his degree in medicine. Dr. Colbert completed his internship and residency with Florida Hospital in Orlando, Florida. He is board certified in family practice and anti-aging medicine and has received extensive training in nutritional medicine.

If you would like more
information about natural and
divine healing, or information about
Divine Health nutritional products,
you may contact Dr. Colbert at:

Don Colbert, MD

1908 Boothe Circle
Longwood, FL 32750
Telephone: 407-331-7007 (for ordering product only)

Dr. Colbert's Web site is
www.drcolbert.com.

Disclaimer: Dr. Colbert and the staff of Divine Health Wellness Center are prohibited from addressing a patient's medical condition by phone, facsimile, or e-mail. Please refer questions related to your medical condition to your own primary care physician.

Pick up these other great Bible Cure books by Don Colbert, MD:

The Bible Cure for ADD and Hyperactivity
The Bible Cure for Allergies
The Bible Cure for Arthritis
The Bible Cure for Asthma
The Bible Cure for Autoimmune Diseases
The Bible Cure for Back Pain
The Bible Cure for Cancer
The Bible Cure for Candida and Yeast Infections
The Bible Cure for Chronic Fatigue and Fibromyalgia
The Bible Cure for Colds, Flu, and Sinus Infections
The Bible Cure for Headaches
The Bible Cure for Heart Disease
The Bible Cure for Heartburn and Indigestion
The Bible Cure for Hepatitis and Hepatitis C
The Bible Cure for High Blood Pressure
The Bible Cure for High Cholesterol
The Bible Cure for Irritable Bowel Syndrome
The Bible Cure for Memory Loss
The Bible Cure for Menopause
The Bible Cure for PMS and Mood Swings
The Bible Cure for Prostate Disorders
The Bible Cure for Skin Disorders
The Bible Cure for Stress
The Bible Cure for Thyroid Disorders
The Bible Cure for Weight Loss and Muscle Gain
The Bible Cure Recipes for Overcoming Candida
The New Bible Cure for Depression and Anxiety
The New Bible Cure for Diabetes
The New Bible Cure for Osteoporosis